God, I Have Issues

50 ways to pray no matter how you feel

MARK E. THIBODEAUX, S.J.

ST. ANTHONY MESSENGER PRESS

Cincinnati, Ohio

Nihil obstat: Paul Deutsch, s.j.
                     September 10, 2004
Imprimi potest: Alfred C. Kammer, s.j.
                     December 1, 2004

Scripture citations, unless otherwise noted, are taken from *New Revised Standard Version Bible*, copyright ©1989 by the Division of Christian Education of the National Council of the Churches of Christ in the U.S.A., and used by permission. All rights reserved.

Cover and book design by Mark Sullivan

Library of Congress Cataloging-in-Publication Data
Thibodeaux, Mark E.
    God, I have issues : 50 ways to pray no matter how you feel / Mark E. Thibodeaux.
        p. cm.
    Includes index.
    ISBN 0-86716-536-7 (alk. paper)
    1. Prayer—Catholic Church—Meditations. 2. Catholic Church—Prayer-books and devotions—English. I. Title.
    BV215.T45 2005
    248.3'2—dc22

                              2004027887
ISBN-13: 978-0-86716-536-4
ISBN-10: 0-86716-536-7

Published by St. Anthony Messenger Press
28 W. Liberty St.
Cincinnati, Ohio 45202
www.SAMPBooks.org

Printed in the U.S.A.

09 10 11 12 13 9 8 7 6

DEDICATION

To my brother Jesuits,
just when I thought I could never find another family as
loving and supportive as my family of origin,
along came you...

ACKNOWLEDGMENTS

Thank you to the Badums, Hernandezes and Parsleys for lending me hideaways, advice and their own comforting and delightful families.

Thank you to Rosi Harmon, Paula Lanousse, Ken Lojo, Gerrie Milgroom, Richard and Nancy Nevle, Carlos Roman, Patricia Yankow, Mary Tarpey, Will Volding and Julie Anne Young for pushing me forward on my moody days when I was ready to say, "God, write your own book!"

Thank you to Lisa Biedenbach, Kathleen Carroll and everyone at St. Anthony Messenger Press. Thank you to Luis Blanco for the page design ideas, to Andy Werner for the data entry and to Mark Bazin for the computer assistance. Without you all, *Issues* would be nothing more than illegible scratches in a coffee-stained notebook.

Thank you to Mom, Dad, Steve, Cameron, Greg, Nancy, Ashley, Dillon, Stuart, Stacey, Abbie, Michael, Eric, Sandy, Marty and Coy for crawfish etouffee, long, slow evenings by a campfire, good sound advice, a thousand funny stories and most especially for unconditional love.

Thank you to my grandmother, Leota Venable, who died just days before I completed this manuscript. You wore Christ's face for all of us, Maw Maw.

Thank you to the entire Strake Jesuit community. I'm so proud to be a part of this amazing place. It makes me want to cry!

Thank you to my Jesuit brothers, a few of whom must be mentioned by name: John Armstrong, Luis Blanco-Döring, Jim Bradley, Jim Caime, Paul Deutsch, Michael Dooley, Raymond Fitzgerald, Randy Gibbens, Tom Greene, Fred Kammer, C. A. Leininger, Larry Lundin, Mark Mossa, David Nantais, Marvin Kitten, Ed Schmidt, Gene Sessa, Gregory Waldrop and Jeremy Zipple. Thank you to the Jesuit Communities of Strake Jesuit,

Loyola of New Orleans, Dallas Jesuit, the Young Jesuit Writers Conference of 2002, the Red Food Group of 2004 and Sacred Heart Retreat House of Sedelia. I beg God to make me worthy of companions like you.

Thank you,

dear Father, my creator,

dear Jesus, my companion,

dear Spirit, my life-breath.

Dear God, may I always strive to give you greater glory.

CONTENTS

Introduction 1

God, I'm Addicted 8

God, I'm Afraid 11

God, I'm Angry 14

God, I'm Angry at You 18

God, I'm in Awe of Your Creation 22

God, I Blew Up Today 26

God, Thank You for My Body 30

God, I'm Too Busy 34

God, I'm Afraid of Change 38

God, I Need to Confront Someone 42

God, I Feel Perfectly Content 46

God, Please Help Me to Decide 50

God, I'm in Despair 54

God, I Have Doubts 58

God, I'm Spiritually Dry 62

God, Someone I Love Is Dying 67

God, It's Evening 72

God, My Family Is Driving Me Nuts! 75

God, I Just Can't Forgive 79

God, I'm Grateful 82

God, I'm Grieving 85

God, I Feel Guilty 89

God, I've Got Bad Habits 92

God, I Hate Myself Today 95

God, I've Been Hurt by Others 98

God, I'm Jealous 101

God, I'm Joyful 104

God, I've Been Judgmental Lately 107

God, I'm Lonely 111

God, I Feel Lost 115

God, I'm in Love 119

God, I'm in Lust 123

God, This Marriage Stuff Is Tough 126

God, This Ministry Stuff Is Tough 130

God, It's Morning 2/1/14 134

God, It's Nighttime 1/23/14 137

God, It's Noontime 140

God, This Parenting Stuff Is Tough 143

God, I'm a Lazy Procrastinator 146

God, I'm Proud of Myself 150

God, I'm Sinfully Proud 153

God, I Feel Still and Quiet 156

God, I'm Sad 160

God, I'm Sexually Aroused 163

God, This Single Life Is Tough 166

God, I've Sinned 169

God, I'm Stressed Out 1/9/14 173

God, I Can't Wait for It 176

God, I'm Weary 3/13/14 180

God, I'm Worried 1/29/14 183

Indexes 187

INTRODUCTION

Speaking to a group of aspiring writers, author and editor Jeremy Langford once said, "Write the book that *you* want to read." Very often as I settle down to pray, I'm preoccupied by a particular mood or situation in my life. I might be filled with joy returning from a family camping trip, or I might be seething with anger about an argument I've just had with my best friend. I might have my dying grandmother in mind, or I simply might want to relax in the stillness of the evening. Often I have a strong sense that God is calling me to bring this mood or situation to our quiet time together. But often, I feel the need for a customized "prayer starter": a Bible passage that deals with my current mood, a short reflection I can use to begin my conversation with God, a concrete suggestion about how to pray in this particular situation or a pithy quote I can easily memorize and carry with me as I exit my prayer and enter my day. Sitting in my prayer chair with coffee mug in hand, I've found myself thinking, "I wish I had a book in which I could look up the mood I'm in today to get me started on my prayer." Searching long and hard for such a book and not finding one, I decided that I ought to take Langford's advice and write one myself.

God, I Have Issues is not intended to be read from cover to cover. It is a reference manual to help you bring the stuff of your life into your daily prayer time. The concept is simple: using the various indexes in the back of the book, find the entry that best fits your situation or mood. You can read the entire entry in the first few minutes of your prayer time and plan your prayer accordingly, meditating on one of the suggested Scriptures, pondering the reflection or trying out one of the prayer pointers.

In the days that follow, you can use the "Suggested Scripture Passages" section to continue your reflections. If you're still needing more, or if this entry does not quite fit your particular situation, you can check out the suggestions from the "Related Entries" section. Finally, you can memorize or scribble down a quote from the "Words to Take with You" section so that you can return to prayer at quiet moments in your day. Some of the quotes are profound and thought provoking, some are just downright silly. But I hope you will find them to be a helpful way of bringing you back to the reflective state of your earlier prayer time.

One caution about this book: these entries are intended for psychologically healthy people going through the typical cycle of everyday emotions and situations. It is far beyond the scope of this book to deal with serious emotional or psychological problems. "God, I'm Sad," for example, is written for the psychologically healthy person who happens to be sad today. A person who is clinically depressed will need to seek professional help and should not rely solely on this or any other spiritual or psychological book for recovery from this serious problem. The same holds for all of the other emotions mentioned in the book.

ABOUT PRAYING WITH THIS BOOK

If you are new to meditation and contemplation, I recommend you take the following three steps:

1. Find two or three good books that are introductions to this
   type of prayer. I recommend one of these:
   > Green, Thomas. *Opening to God.* (Ave Maria Press, 1977.)
   > Hauser, Richard. *In His Spirit.* (Paulist Press, 1982.)
   > Keating, Thomas. *Intimacy with God.*
   > (Crossroad/Herder & Herder, 1996.)

Link, Mark. *The Challenge 2000* Series. (Thomas More
Press, 1993.)
Thibodeaux, Mark. *Armchair Mystic: Easing Into
Contemplative Prayer.* (St. Anthony Messenger Press,
2001.)
Zanzig, Thomas. *Learning to Meditate.* (St. Mary's Press,
1990.)

2. Find a spiritual director, someone who has more experience
   in contemplation and mediation, who can guide you as you
   take your first steps and can help you maintain a healthy
   prayer life once you've been at it for a while.
3. Find at least one or two peers with whom you can share your
   spiritual journeys, exchange insights, ideas and so on.

Here's a simple formula for using this book in a daily regimen
of prayer:

Find a quiet time and space in which to pray every day.
Many pray-ers find the best *time* to pray to be the early
morning and the best *place* to pray to be a chair that is comfortable but not so much so that one would fall asleep easily. Beside your chair, place whatever helps you to pray: a
Bible, a candle, a journal and pen, a spiritual book.

Before beginning prayer, ask yourself what topic, emotion,
issues or situation God and you might want to work with
today. On some days nothing in particular will come to
mind. You may want to pray over the liturgical readings of
the day or simply have a cup of coffee with Jesus. On other
days some particular mood, situation or issue might be very
present to you. If so, look up the mood or situation in the
book and quickly read over the entire entry. Place the book
open-faced beside your chair.

Begin to quiet yourself. Slow down your breathing. Settle
down your thoughts. You might want to hum a simple

religious tune or speak a mantra, a holy word or phrase, over and over again. For example, you might want to say the name "Jesus" very slowly over and over again. Allow yourself to sit in this holy stillness for as long as it feels comfortable.

If you feel yourself coming out of that stillness and if it feels right to do so, pick up this book and again skim the entire entry. When you find something that strikes you, ignore all the rest and focus on that one part. For example, if a particular Scripture passage looks appealing, look up that passage and pray over it for the entire prayer period. Or perhaps something in the reflection will strike you; then stay with that thought or insight and have a conversation with God about it. Or perhaps you'll want to try out one of the "Prayer Pointers." Whatever you choose to pray with, it is important that you do not clutter your prayer time with activities or even multiple Scripture passages. It is far better to focus on one small point, insight or passage than to jump from one spot to another.

Close your prayer time with the Lord's Prayer, the Glory Be to the Father or some other ready-made prayer. Before leaving your prayer spot, you might want to consider what you'll pray over tomorrow. You might also memorize one of the quotes from "Words to Take with You" or scribble it on a slip of paper so that you can go back to it here and there during your day.

ABOUT PRAYING WITH SCRIPTURE

Those who practice Christian meditation and contemplation find praying with Scriptures to be the bread and butter of their prayer life. Therefore, each entry provides a list of "Suggested Scripture Passages." In preparing to pray, you might want to peruse the list and look up the passages that seem promising.

Settle down with one passage and bookmark that spot in your Bible before beginning to pray. That way you won't have to distract yourself with finding the right passage and flipping to it during the prayer time itself.

Saint Ignatius Loyola suggests that once you have found a passage that really works in prayer (that is, one that helps you get in touch with God), then you should stay with that passage for as long as it continues to work. If the passage really speaks to you or moves you closer to God, you might pray over the same passage again and again for several days or even weeks. The goal then is *not* to pray over every single passage relating to your mood or situation, but instead to pray deeply over one or, at most, a few passages.

In the same way that you shouldn't try to cover every passage, you might find it more helpful to focus on *one small part* of one passage. Psalm 139:1–18, for example, is a rich passage filled with many wonderful words, phrases and images. Instead of trying to cover them all in your prayer time, it would be better to choose the one word, phrase or image that speaks to you today and zero in on that one, leaving all the rest of it behind.

Here are three concrete ways to meditate on Scripture:

Ask a reflection question. Read the passage and think of a reflection question to discuss with God. Basically, ask God and yourself, "What is this passage about?" and, "How does this relate to my life?"

Play a role in the story. Read the Bible story several times and, in your imagination, play the role of one of the characters in the story. Then have a talk with Jesus about what you experienced.

Use a mantra. The mantra is a word, phrase or sentence that you repeat over and over. Simply pick your favorite line from the passage and very slowly, very prayerfully, say that word, phrase or sentence over and over again. Let it take root in your heart.

ABOUT PRAYING WITH EMOTIONS

Why should I pray over my emotions? For the most part, emotions are amoral. That is to say, at least to the extent that I don't choose the particular emotion I'm now experiencing, they are neither virtuous nor sinful. Very often, good people make the mistake of trying (either unconsciously or consciously) to repress emotions they consider "bad" or "sinful." For example, if I were married, I may unconsciously hold to this fallacy: "I must suppress all feelings of anger toward my wife because good husbands feel love and affection for their spouses all the time." The problem is that repressing or suppressing my emotions does not make them go away. On the contrary, strong emotions that are not dealt with straightforwardly will seek some sort of unconscious release. For example, unrepressed anger toward my spouse might lead me to passive-aggressive behavior such as "forgetting" to take care of responsibilities around the house or, even worse, making "harmless jokes" about her to my friends.

So if emotions must be dealt with, then how should I do so? Should I simply scream at the wife anytime I feel angry? Of course not. I can consciously choose for myself how I will release these emotions, but doing so requires reflection and temperance. This is where prayer comes in. If I pray about the strong emotions I'm feeling, God and I can find healthy ways of expressing and releasing them. Oftentimes, simply consciously acknowledging them before God is enough of a release and nothing more is required. At other times I might need to take some concrete action. At those times I will have to discern what is the right action—what is God's will for me. Returning to the example of spousal anger, it may be the case that acknowledging that anger before God is all that is needed. I may in my prayer time feel a sense of relief and release once I have talked it over with God. On the other hand, God might challenge me to deal with deeper problems at the root of my anger. God might reveal to me that the anger is an emotional problem I must come to terms with in my life. Or I might discern that my anger is pointing to an issue in my marriage that needs to be tended to by both my wife and me. God and I could discern then how best to approach my wife with this problem. Whatever the case may be, praying about the persistent emotions in my life will only help me to grow and become a more mature and loving person.

There is another related reason why it's a great idea to pray with my emotions. The core of our Christian faith is our belief in an incarnate God. We believe that God loves us so much that he became one of us. He desired so much to be part of our lives that he stepped into the murky waters of humanity. Through Jesus Christ, he enters into the nitty-gritty of our lives. He is not satisfied with standing on the sidelines, cheering us when we score and bandaging us when we get hurt. No, God chooses to get in the game! And through the Holy Spirit, he chooses to get in *my* game. The Spirit of God wants to join me in all of my joys and sorrows, my quiet days and my raucous ones, too. But out of love, the Spirit of God respects my free will and does not enter where he is not invited. Praying over emotions, then, is saying yes to God's offer to enter into my very heart. "Listen! I am at the door knocking," says Jesus. "If you hear my voice and open the door, I will come in to you and eat with you, and you with me" (Revelation 3:20).

GOD, I'M ADDICTED

...to keep me from being too elated, a thorn was given me
in the flesh, a messenger of Satan to torment me, to keep
me from being too elated. Three times I appealed to the
Lord about this, that it would leave me, but he said to me,
"My grace is sufficient for you, for power is made perfect
in weakness." So, I will boast all the more gladly of my
weaknesses, so that the power of Christ may dwell in me.
—2 Corinthians 12:7–9

In God's eyes, addictions are avenues for salvation. They provide the impetus I need to finally surrender my life to God. My
addiction is "exhibit A" among my proofs for why I can't manage the job of being my own savior. I have many other proofs,
but this one is the most convincing. Without my addiction, I
could almost convince myself that I don't need a savior. But try
as I might, no matter what I do, no matter how many degrees I
get, or how many friends I have, or how many promises I make,
or how many times a day I pray, I cannot get a handle on my
addiction. I am powerless over it. I will need a higher power to
rescue me from it.

Some of the happiest, healthiest, holiest people I know are
alcoholics who speak freely of their addiction. It is as though
they have found some sort of freedom in being able to say, "I
give up. I can't handle it, and I won't fight it anymore. I'm an
alcoholic: I am powerless in the face of alcohol." I can't imagine the relief one must feel in being able to finally let go of the
battles and ask Christ to be one's champion. Many will even go
so far as to say that they are *grateful* for their addiction, for it was
through it that they found God and even found themselves.
Sounds a lot like Saint Paul, doesn't it?

I will boast all the more gladly of my weaknesses,
so that the power of Christ may dwell in me.
(2 Corinthians 12:9)

Every one of us is an addict. Every one of us clings too tightly to one thing or another. If we're not careful, our addictions will destroy us. They may flatten us quickly, or they may corrode our lives little by little, leaving us impotent and lifeless. That is, of course, if we choose not to use our addictions to lead us to the altar of Christ—the place where we Christians *celebrate* the broken body of our Lord. It is in that brokenness that we are made whole.

ADDICTED

SUGGESTED SCRIPTURE PASSAGES

EXODUS 32: The golden calf
NUMBERS 11: Complaining in the desert
JUDGES 16:4–31: Samson's lust destroys him
1 KINGS 11: Solomon turns his heart to other gods
EZEKIEL 37:1–14: God restores dry bones
JOEL 2:15—3:2: Call to penance; the Lord responds
MATTHEW 17:14–21: Casting out demons
MATTHEW 19:16–30: The rich young man
MARK 5:1–20: The healing of the demoniac
MARK 5:21–43: Fear is useless—what is needed is faith
MARK 10:46–52: The blind man Bartimaeus
LUKE 12:13–21: Storing up earthly treasure
LUKE 23:39–43: Jesus saves the good thief
JOHN 4:1–39: The woman at the well
JOHN 8:1–11: The woman being stoned
JOHN 8:31–36: The truth will set you free
ROMANS 7:14–25: What I want to do, I do not do
2 CORINTHIANS 4:7–18: We are afflicted but not crushed
2 CORINTHIANS 12:7–10: My grace is sufficient for you

ADDICTED

PRAYER POINTERS

If I have not already done so, I pray over the Twelve Steps of Alcoholics Anonymous (see www.aa.org). I spend a great deal of time reflecting on my powerlessness in the face of my addiction. I beg God to take over my life—to be my savior.

I ask God, "Of these twelve steps, which do I need to work on the most right now?" God and I have a conversation about this.

I prayerfully search for one person with whom I can share my troubles. I consider well who would be the most helpful to me. I imagine myself telling this person absolutely everything about my addiction, and I imagine how this person might respond. I consider committing myself to actually approaching this person about it.

RELATED ENTRIES

Habits, Hate, Guilty, Lust, Sinned

WORDS TO TAKE WITH YOU

A sick dog always returns to his vomit.
—Proverbs 26:11 (paraphrased)

Worms become butterflies.
—Anonymous

God did not invite the Children of Israel to leave the slavery of Egypt: he commanded them to do so.
—Thomas Merton

The truth has many enemies. The lie has many friends.
—Bartolome de Las Casas

Those who lie with dogs rise with fleas.
—Blackfoot Proverb

GOD, I'M AFRAID

When it was evening on that day, the first day of the week, and the doors of the house where the disciples had met were locked for fear of the Jews, Jesus came and stood among them and said, "Peace be with you." After he said this, he showed them his hands and his side. Then the disciples rejoiced when they saw the Lord. Jesus said to them again, "Peace be with you. As the Father has sent me, so I send you." When he had said this, he breathed on them and said to them, "Receive the Holy Spirit...."
—John 20:19–22

Prayer can help me to get to the roots of my fear. For example, if I feel frightened by the notion of speaking out against some unjust practice at work, I'll want to ask myself, "What am I really afraid of? Rejection by my peers? Rejection by my superiors? Am I afraid of conflict itself? Am I afraid of losing my job?"

Each day that I pray over this situation, I want to dig deeper into my fears. Each time I ask the question, "What am I really afraid of?", I should try to discover a deeper answer. Using the example above, I may discover after a number of prayer times that I am afraid of my boss. I then want to ask myself again, "What is it about my boss that I'm really afraid of?" I may then discover that my boss reminds me of my overbearing mother who disciplined me through fear. Or, I may feel a need to impress my boss and am afraid to get on her bad side. Or, I may realize that I feel my job is constantly threatened—that the boss could fire me at any moment. If losing my job is the fear, I may come back and ask the question again, "What is it I'm really afraid of?" I may discover that beneath the fear of losing my job is a terrible fear of being an inadequate father. Now we're getting somewhere! But I haven't arrived at this root cause of my fear until after I have spent a great deal of time in prayer, asking myself again and again, "What am I really afraid of?"

The next step, of course, would be to allow Jesus to enter that scary place with me. My friend Paul once told me of a prayer experience whereby he and Jesus were walking through the many rooms of his house—a metaphor for his very self. After a while they came to a locked door that represented Paul's most frightening parts of himself, and he said to Jesus, "Sorry, Lord, I can't let you in that door." For several prayer times more, Paul reflected on how much of his emotional and spiritual life is spent guarding that door—keeping everyone, including Jesus and even himself, from entering it. You can imagine the liberation Paul finally experienced when he gathered up the courage to walk into that room with Jesus.

I must do the same. I must take Jesus' hand and walk into my own dark, cobwebbed room. I sit on the floor awhile with him and get a feel for this place I've run from for so long. I let Jesus light a candle, so that we can see it clearly and describe it to one another. Now that the light is on, is this place so scary after all?

SUGGESTED SCRIPTURE PASSAGES

1 SAMUEL 17:32–51: David and Goliath

PSALM 23: The Lord is my shepherd, I shall not want

PSALM 27: The Lord is my light and my salvation

PSALM 56: When I'm afraid, I put my trust in you

PSALM 62: My soul rests in God alone

PSALM 69: Save me, O God

PSALM 91: He will rescue you from the snare of the fowler

PSALM 118: The Lord is with me; I fear not

ISAIAH 25:4—26:4: The Lord is an eternal rock

ISAIAH 41:1–10: Fear not, for I am with you

ISAIAH 43:1–8: You will walk through fire, and not be burned

MATTHEW 10:16–20: Don't worry about what to say

MATTHEW 14:22–33: Jesus rescues the apostles
from the stormy sea

MARK 5:21–43: Fear is useless—what is needed is faith
MARK 10:27: All things are possible with God
MARK 16:1–8: The women fled from the tomb
LUKE 10:38–42: Martha, you are anxious about many things
LUKE 22:40–46: Jesus sweats blood in the
garden of Gethsemane
JOHN 20:19–23: The resurrected Christ says,
"Peace be with you"
ACTS 4:1–31: The Holy Spirit comes to help Peter
ROMANS 8:28–39: All things work together for the good
2 CORINTHIANS 12:7–10: My grace is sufficient for you
1 PETER 5:6–11: Cast all your cares on him,
for he cares for you
1 JOHN 4:18: Cast out all fear

AFRAID

PRAYER POINTERS

I allow Jesus and me to explore ever deeper levels of the roots of my fear. With each new level of response to Jesus' question, "What are you *really* afraid of?" I write a detailed description of my fears.

Using my friend Paul's metaphor, I imagine each of the levels of response as rooms within rooms. At each new room I draw a detailed picture of Jesus and me inside the room. I speak with Jesus about the images that are being conjured up in my mind.

RELATED ENTRIES

Confront, Nighttime, Worried

WORDS TO TAKE WITH YOU

I know that God will not give me anything that I can't handle.
I just wish he didn't trust me so much.
—Mother Teresa of Calcutta

GOD, I'M ANGRY

> When the days drew near for him to be taken up, he set his face to go to Jerusalem. And he sent messengers ahead of him. On their way they entered a village of the Samaritans to make ready for him; but they did not receive him, because his face was set toward Jerusalem. When his disciples James and John saw it, they said, "Lord, do you want us to command fire to come down from heaven and consume them?" But he turned and rebuked them. Then they went on to another village.
> —Luke 9:51–55

I have *righteous anger* when I have been unjustifiably wronged and am justifiably angry about it. In and of itself, righteous anger is amoral; it is neither sinful nor virtuous. It has some good qualities. For example, it was righteous anger that led Candy Lightner, an angry mother whose daughter was killed by a drunk driver, to start the group Mothers Against Drunk Driving, which works to end drunk driving in America.

But righteous anger can be dangerous. Psychologically speaking, it is a defense mechanism I use to give me power when I feel powerless in the face of some evil done to me. If I'm not careful, I can become addicted to the power it brings me. I can stew in the delicious strength I feel from the rage inside me. If I do not ultimately let it go, it will consume me over time.

If anyone had a right to have righteous anger, it would be the crucified Jesus. He was purely innocent and yet died a savage and brutal death. But instead of being angry, as he hangs in excruciating pain, Jesus cries out, "Father, forgive them, for they know not what they do." Spiritual writer Thomas Hart humorously points out that, for the apostles, the appearance of the resurrected Jesus might not necessarily be a good thing. After all, how would you feel if the friend that you had betrayed and abandoned came back from the dead to see you? Jesus had every right to be furious with his apostles—to say, "Where were you? After all I've done for you!" But instead, Jesus granted them amnesty: "Peace is my gift to you," he said.

Perhaps this is part of what it means to be resurrected: to relinquish one's right to be angry and to wish and work for peace on earth and good will toward all, even toward one's perpetrators. Until we reach this point, we will still be mortally wounded.

The New Testament says that God the Father raised Jesus from the dead. If this is true about Jesus, this will certainly be true for us, too. We cannot resurrect ourselves; we must let God raise us. And like Jesus, we must spend some time in the tomb. We must wait for the gift to come. The question is, "What will we do with this anger in the meantime?"

SUGGESTED SCRIPTURE PASSAGES

GENESIS 27:1–45; 33:1–20: Jacob and Esau
GENESIS 37:1–36; 42:1—45:28: The story of Joseph
MATTHEW 21:18–22: Jesus curses the fig tree
MATTHEW 23:1–39: Jesus versus the Pharisees
MARK 8:31–33: Jesus to Peter: "Get away from me, Satan!"
JOHN 2:13–25: Jesus cleanses the temple
JOHN 21:1–25: Jesus forgives Peter
EPHESIANS 4:25–32: Do not let the sun go down
on your anger

PRAYER POINTERS

After reaching stillness, I imagine myself sitting in one of three chairs in an empty room. I ask myself, "Who is the person whom I am most angry with at this moment? My brother? My spouse? My boss? Why am I angry with him or her? What am I feeling deep down in my heart about him or her?" I do not settle on the first answers that I come up with. I keep probing—asking myself these questions until I feel I have reached the core of the issues.

I then imagine that very person sitting in one of the empty chairs. I imagine this person telling me everything he or she is feeling about me and about the present situation. I imagine this person speaking without fear, anxiety or embarrassment. What would he or she say? I listen quietly and attentively to the words spoken.

I now share with this person what I have discovered are my deep emotions right now. I imagine myself without fear, anxiety or embarrassment and able to say exactly what I am feeling. If I need to yell and scream at him or her for a while, I go for it. Again, I say exactly what I'm feeling without any censorship.

I now notice Jesus sitting in the third chair and listening intently to our conversation. I ask him to share with me his feelings about this situation. What does he say? Is he happy? Disappointed? Does he have some insight the other two of us haven't thought of? What is my response? How should my attitude and actions toward this person change because of this encounter with Jesus?

I allow a three-way conversation to continue, allowing everyone a chance to say anything he or she wishes.

If I'm really angry right now, I may have to pray about this for a while. Each time I pray this prayer time, I end it by telling this person that I love him or her regardless of how I feel right now. It is extremely important that I end the prayer time with words of love for this person. If my heart is not ready to say these words, I let my will do the talking. My heart will come along in its own good time.

RELATED ENTRIES

Blew Up, Confront, Family, Forgive, Hurt, Judgmental, Marriage, Parenting

WORDS TO TAKE WITH YOU

Hate and bitterness are the only weapons wielded by the blade.
—Thomas Gregory

ANGRY

GOD, I'M ANGRY AT YOU

Those who passed by derided him, shaking their heads and saying, "Aha! You who would destroy the temple and build it in three days, save yourself, and come down from the cross!" In the same way the chief priests, along with the scribes, were also mocking him among themselves and saying, "He saved others; he cannot save himself. Let the Messiah, the King of Israel, come down from the cross now, so that we may see and believe." Those who were crucified with him also taunted him.

When it was noon, darkness came over the whole land until three in the afternoon. At three o'clock Jesus cried out with a loud voice, "Eloi, Eloi, lema sabachthani?" which means, "My God, my God, why have you forsaken me?"

—Mark 15:29–34

Many Christians fear that God will punish or eternally damn them if they slip up and say the wrong thing to him. But is this an image of an all-loving God? Would I want such a person as a friend? A spouse? A teacher? A parent? God is not like this at all. If I want a good image of God, I should think of the most loving and compassionate person in my life and imagine God to be infinitely *more* loving and compassionate. Furthermore, God desires that we have an *intimate relationship* with him. And because I am human, I naturally will have problems in this relationship. I will get angry with God as I sometimes get angry with my spouse, my friend, my parents and so on.

The Bible is filled with examples of friends of God who at one time or another got angry with him. Sarah cynically laughed at God's promise that she and Abraham would have a child in their old age. Jacob wrestled with an angel for a blessing. The Israelites in the desert complained about the food. In the New Testament, though Jesus was divine, his best friends often argued with him. Here are a few examples:

"Lord, we have been fishing all day and have caught nothing. Now you're telling us to go back out there?"

"OK, fine. Let's go to Jerusalem to die with Jesus."

"If you had been here, Lazarus would not have died."

"Do you not care, Lord, that we're all going to die?"

"Lord, if we have no idea where you are going, how can we follow?"

"If I have to die for you Lord, will your beloved disciple have to die, too?"

And Jesus himself, at the most important moment of his life, shouted at God, "My God, my God, why have you abandoned me?"

Perhaps the best example of a healthy conflict with God is that of Old Testament hero Job, who for chapters and chapters shook his fist at God. Biblical scholars say that the vocabulary of much of Job's ranting implies that Job actually wanted to take God to court. He wanted to convict God in a heavenly court of law. When Job made that seemingly beautiful statement, "I know that my Redeemer lives" (Job 19:25), he actually was referring to a heavenly being who could help him to convict God in this celestial trial!

In every one of these examples, God remained faithful and did not condemn the angry follower. At times God fought back, but only when it would help the person to grow. Sarah bore a child and became the mother of the Judeo-Christian world. Jacob got his blessing. The Israelites were given the Promised Land. Peter became pope. And Job, having lost his court battle, was blessed with riches and great wisdom.

So, if you have a beef with God, what are you waiting for? Go after him!

SUGGESTED SCRIPTURE PASSAGES

EXODUS 5: Lord, you have not rescued your people
NUMBERS 11:10–15: Lord, why have you treated me so badly?
JOB 7:11–19: I will complain in the bitterness of my soul
JOB 19:23–27: I know that my Redeemer lives
PSALM 22: My God, why have you forsaken me?
PSALM 88: Lord, my soul is full of troubles
JEREMIAH 20:7–18: You duped me, O Lord
LAMENTATIONS 3: I have seen affliction
JONAH 4: Jonah's anger at the Lord's compassion
MARK 4:35–41: Do you not care that we're going to die?
JOHN 11:1–44: Martha: "Lord, if you had been here…"
HEBREWS 12:5–13: Lift your drooping hands and
strengthen weak knees

PRAYER POINTERS

Looking at these various biblical characters, I notice that some of God's best friends were sometimes furious with him. And they seemed to have no trouble letting God know that they were angry! With this assurance, I go after God. I sit him in the chair in front of me and I let him have it, telling him every little thing that is bothering me about him right now. I hold nothing back and say everything that comes to mind.

If I feel more comfortable doing so, I write God a nasty letter giving him a piece of my mind. Point by point, I spell out all the ways I feel that he has screwed up my life. Again, I hold nothing back.

Throughout my ranting, I imagine God sitting quietly and listening with great care and great love. When I have exhausted myself with all that I've had to say, I sit quietly and allow God to respond. I let God say or do anything he wants. Perhaps he will reach out to embrace me. Perhaps he will respond to my particular problems, pointing out his logic. Perhaps he will simply ask me to trust. Perhaps he will yell back! Perhaps he will remain silent and distant.

I respond to God in whatever way feels natural. I may need to yell some more. I may need to melt in his arms. I may need to keep my distance for a while. I may need to ask questions. I allow myself to say or do whatever my heart leads me to do.

If I am really angry with God, there is a good chance that I will have to pray about this for a long time. At the end of each prayer time, I tell God that I love him and accept his will for me in my life and trust that his will is always what is best for me. If my heart cannot say these words right now, I let my own will do the talking for me.

ANGRY AT YOU

RELATED ENTRIES

Angry, Dry, Grieving, Ministry

WORDS TO TAKE WITH YOU

I chased him until he caught me.
—Anonymous

Dear Lord, if this is how you treat your friends, it is no wonder you have so few!
—Saint Teresa of Avila

GOD, I'M IN AWE OF YOUR CREATION

Frost and chill, bless the Lord.
—Daniel 3:69 (NAB)

Praised be you, my Lord, with all your creatures, especially Sir Brother Sun, Who is the day and through whom you give us light. And he is beautiful and radiant with great splendor....
—Saint Francis of Assisi

Everyone in the course of a lifetime experiences rare and wonderful epiphanies in nature when God momentarily lifts the veil of our unknowing and shows us his face. Here's one of mine:

January, 2000

At approximately six o'clock this morning, I put on my running gear and ran six miles along the Charles River in Cambridge, Massachusetts. The temperature was in the upper teens or lower twenties! I almost turned around at several points in the first few minutes of the run. My hands were so cold that I had to keep twirling my fingers just to keep the circulation going. My strange high-tech running suit managed to cover practically every part of me. But there was a small, one-inch triangle of flesh at the bottom of my neck where the zipper of my suit did not come all the way up to meet my ski mask. In that biting cold, I was introduced to this small spot on my body that I had never noticed before. When I reached the frozen river, I saw the Boston skyline in a gradually more oranging sky and was grateful that I had not turned around and missed this.

A little farther on, the trail left Storrow Drive and went through a park area where all I saw were trees on my right and the river on my left. While running beside it, I spent a while observing the thin sheet of ice that had formed on the surface of the river. Twenty minutes into the run, I emerged from a particularly engrossing and absorbing conversation with God to realize—to my great surprise—that I was no longer cold. All body parts were warm and comfortable—even my newfound little spot! I was awestruck at my body's ability to regulate its own temperature, even in these conditions. Fifty minutes into the run, I had come full circle and was home again—happy that it was over, but a little sad, too. Like Adam in the fresco on the wall of the Sistine Chapel, for just a moment I felt the touch of God on my flesh.

So, what's your story?

SUGGESTED SCRIPTURE PASSAGES

GENESIS 1:1—2:4: The creation story
JOB 38–41: The Lord speaks of his creation
PSALM 8: The Lord's majesty
PSALM 29: The God of glory thunders over mighty waters
PSALM 104: Bless the Lord, O my soul
PSALM 145: One generation shall laud your works to another
DANIEL 3:52–90: All things bless the Lord
MATTHEW 6:25–34: Consider the lilies
COLOSSIANS 1:3–20: By him, all things were created

PRAYER POINTERS

If I am currently experiencing one of these moments of epiphany with nature, then I bask in the wonder of it. I stay with that moment as long as possible. I sit in the leaves, climb the tree, wade in the river. Through it all, I recognize the Creator's

AWE OF YOUR CREATION

presence in the very essence of his creation, and I praise God for it.

I read slowly through Daniel 3:52–90 and then write my own stanzas to reflect my own personal experience (for example, "Leaf and tree, praise the Lord. Mockingbird and mosquito, praise the Lord").

I record this moment in my journal. I write a poem or a song about it. I paint a picture or mold a sculpture with clay. I take some memento of the moment (a leaf, a pebble) and place it next to my computer or on the kitchen windowsill; I allow that little object to take me back to the place several times throughout my day.

I respond to God's awesome gift of creation by letting God know how overwhelmed I am by its beauty and grace. Perhaps I will make some commitment to God as a response to this divine gift of creation.

RELATED ENTRIES

Body, Content, Evening, Grateful, Joyful, Love, Quiet

WORDS TO TAKE WITH YOU

Earth's crammed with heaven and every common bush afire
with God; and only he who sees takes off his shoes.
—Elizabeth Barrett Browning

Glory be to God for dappled things
For skies of couple-colour as a brinded cow;
For rose-moles all in stipple upon trout that swim;
Fresh-firecoal chestnut-falls; finches' wings;
Landscape plotted and pieced—fold, fallow, and plough;
And all trades, their gear and tackle and trim.
All things counter, original, spare, strange;

AWE OF YOUR CREATION

Whatever is fickle, freckled (who knows how?)
With swift, slow; sweet, sour; adazzle, dim;
He fathers-forth whose beauty is past change:
Praise him.
—"Pied Beauty," Gerard Manley Hopkins, s.j.

AWE OF YOUR CREATION

GOD, I BLEW UP TODAY

Cain said to his brother Abel, "Let us go out to the field." And when they were in the field, Cain rose up against his brother Abel, and killed him. Then the LORD said to Cain, "Where is your brother Abel?" He said, "I do not know; am I my brother's keeper?" And the LORD said, "What have you done? Listen; your brother's blood is crying out to me from the ground...."
—Genesis 4:8–10

There are rare occasions when blowing up is the right thing to do. Sometimes I'm called by God to shake people out of their traditional way of thinking or acting. I must be the one to stop the speeding train from careening over a cliff, and the only way to do so is to crash into it head-on myself. As a teacher, a parent, a friend, a leader, a citizen, a church member, I am sometimes called to stand up and turn over the tables of the moneychangers. The only good motive for ever doing so is love. I decide that the most loving thing that I can do at this moment is to destroy the comfortable godless world in which people are dwelling.

But those times are rare. Most of the time when I blow up, it's because I've lost control of my own passions, and I explode like an erupted pressure cooker.

Why do people explode in anger? A friend of mine who is active in Alcoholics Anonymous taught me the H.A.L.T. formula. She said, "When you're about to blow up and do something stupid, you've got to H.A.L.T. and ask yourself, 'Am I *H*ungry? Am I *A*ngry? Am I *L*onely? Am I *T*ired?' Once you've determined which of these four is the problem, you can work on fixing that relatively simple need rather than losing control and behaving destructively."

From another perspective, science tells us that every species of animal in the world generally reacts to perceived threats in one of two ways: fight or flight. When I'm courageous enough to pray about my outbursts of anger, I often discover that the motive behind the outburst was not love at all but rather some unacknowledged fear deep inside me. Often, when I explode, it's because, far below the level of consciousness, I feel terribly threatened, and I am desperately trying to save myself.

Should this be the case, then, in my prayer, as I look back on my outburst, I must courageously allow Jesus to ask me, "What did you feel threatened by?" That's a tough question to face. If I exploded emotionally, it's probably because of a deep-seated pain. It will not reveal its frightened self easily. I will have to approach it gingerly, carefully, slowly. I must beg God to give me the strength and the courage to face this wound with integrity and humility. Once I've confronted my threatened self, I can then ask Christ to begin the slow process of healing me. On a practical level, I can seek ways to feel more secure in similar situations.

SUGGESTED SCRIPTURE PASSAGES

GENESIS 4:1–15: Cain kills Abel

PSALM 103: The Lord is slow to anger and
abounding in steadfast love

PSALM 131: O Lord, my soul is still

PROVERBS 14:17: A quick tempered man does foolish things

ISAIAH 2:2–5: They shall beat their swords into plowshares

MATTHEW 5:21–26: Everyone who grows angry shall
be liable to judgment

MATTHEW 5:38–43: Love your enemies

MATTHEW 21:18–22: Jesus curses the fig tree

MATTHEW 26:47–56: The one who lives by the sword
shall die by the sword

MARK 11:15–19: Jesus cleanses the temple

BLEW UP

LUKE 9:51–56: Jesus chides the apostles about their revenge
JOHN 2:13–25: Jesus and the moneychangers
ACTS 15: Paul and Barnabas fight and split
ROMANS 12:17–21: "Vengeance is mine," says the Lord
EPHESIANS 4:25–32: Do not let the sun go down on your anger
JAMES 3: No one can tame the tongue—
a restless evil, full of poison

PRAYER POINTERS

As painful as it is to do so, I pray for those who hurt me and for those whom I have hurt. I ask the Lord to bless these people with his abundant love and grace.

If I have blown up recently, it would be good for me to practice stillness in my prayer. I should ask the Lord for the grace of inner peace. Praying over Psalm 131 or using a mantra such as "Still me, O Lord" might help.

Sometimes I discover in my prayer that I feel threatened by a particular person. In my journal, I write him or her a letter that I never intend to send. That way, I can be uncensored in laying down my own vulnerability and fear. The purpose of this letter is *not* to reconcile with the person, but rather to get in touch with my own fear. By addressing the letter to the person whom I fear, I am beginning the slow process of facing him or her. After I have written the letter, I should read it aloud to Jesus and ask him for consolation and healing. Only then can Jesus and I begin to discern how to reconcile with that person.

After praying over the question, "What am I threatened by?", I might also explore the following questions: "Would it be appropriate for me to attempt to reconcile with those I may have hurt? If so, how? Am I ready to forgive myself for losing it? Do those I've hurt know that I love them? Is there an appropriate way of expressing my love at this time?"

Lord, make me an instrument of your peace.
Where there is hatred, let me sow love;
where there is injury, pardon;
where there is doubt, faith;
where there is despair, hope;
where there is darkness, light;
where there is sadness, joy.
Grant that I may not so much seek
to be consoled as to console;
to be understood as to understand;
to be loved as to love.
it is in giving that we receive;
it is in pardoning that we are pardoned;
and it is in dying that we are born to eternal life.
—Peace Prayer of Saint Francis

RELATED ENTRIES

Angry, Confront, Guilty, Hurt by Others,
Judgmental, Marriage, Sinned

WORDS TO TAKE WITH YOU

Sure the world breeds monsters, but kindness grows
just as wild.
—Mary Karr

Be kind, for everyone you meet is fighting a harder battle.
—Plato

Better to remain silent and appear stupid, than to speak
and eliminate all doubt.
—Anonymous

GOD, THANK YOU FOR MY BODY

I praise you, for I am fearfully and wonderfully made.
    Wonderful are your works;
that I know very well.
    My frame was not hidden from you,
when I was being made in secret,
    intricately woven in the depths of the earth.
Your eyes beheld my unformed substance.
In your book were written
    all the days that were formed for me,
    when none of them as yet existed.
—Psalm 139:14–16

One lazy summer day a couple of years ago, I was playing with my nephews, Cameron and Dillon. They were taking turns doing tricks on Cameron's new scooter. It looked easy to ride (famous last words), so I said, "Let me give it a try." It took about twenty seconds for me to flip over the thing, careening into the mud. Afterward, I noticed that I had a fairly large cut on my leg from my wipeout. I cleaned it up and forgot about it.

A few days later, I spent five days alone in the hill country of Texas so that I could write without distraction. During those reflective days, I was unusually observant of the healing process of that cut. I watched in awe as the cut grew uglier and more "colorful," then gradually more natural-looking and harmless. One day I noticed perfectly smooth and unblemished pink skin all around it. It stirred me to consider the ease with which my body could recover from injury and "create" entirely new and perfect parts of itself. Now, weeks later, there is only the tiniest of scars left. A part of me wonders if my body could have gotten rid of even the scar but chose to keep it around in order to remind me that I'm a little too old now for scooters!

I have always been fascinated by the phenomenon of homeostasis, the body's ability to maintain balance and equilibrium in all of its systems. Many bodily functions that we consider problems are actually solutions from the perspective of the body. It is the body, not the disease, that causes fever. It does so because many bacteria cannot survive at higher temperatures. The body causes vomiting when it detects poison in the system and wants to flush itself clean. Sometimes headaches occur because the body, sensing that oxygen levels in the brain are a little low, rushes more of it upward. Homeostasis also refers to the unbelievable ability to keep my body temperature almost precisely the same whether I go for a run in the eleven-degree cold of Cambridge, Massachusetts, or in the ninety-one-degree heat of Houston, Texas.

Now, how can that be? How can I be created so marvelously? It takes my breath away just to think about what an amazing wonder is this clumsy, beat-up, slightly overweight body of mine. When I praise the Lord, I do so for the gifts of family, vocation, friends, granted favors and undeserved graces. But how often do I sit in awe of the giftedness of my thumb, of the industry of my digestive system, of the particularity of my pinky-toe?

> I praise you, for I am fearfully and wonderfully made. (Psalm 139:14)

SUGGESTED SCRIPTURE PASSAGES

GENESIS 1:1—2:4: God looked at what he made
and saw that it was good
PSALM 139:1–18: I praise you, for I am wonderfully made
ECCLESIASTES 1:1—2:26: Vanity of vanities; all is vanity
WISDOM 11:24–25: You love all you made
HOSEA 11:1–4: When Israel was a child, I loved him
MATTHEW 6:25–34: Consider the lilies
LUKE 12:22–32: Do not worry about what you are to wear
LUKE 17:11–19: The grateful leper

1 CORINTHIANS 6:15–20: The body is a temple
1 CORINTHIANS 15:35–58: Our resurrected bodies

PRAYER POINTERS

I find a sitting position that is comfortable, but not so much so that I will fall asleep easily. A cushioned chair that forces me to sit up straight usually does the trick. In the long run, breathing is easier and more relaxed when I'm sitting up. I sit quietly a few moments, allowing my breathing to slow down and my body to relax.

Without moving and in that same quiet state, I focus all of my attention on the big toe of my right foot. I "sense" the presence of that toe as I never have before. I feel its contentment with simply "being" there at the end of my foot. In my heart I say to God repeatedly, "Thank you, Lord." After a while, I move on to my entire right foot. I note its peacefulness and tranquility—its lack of anxiety or fear. I say again, "Thank you, Lord."

I now allow its partner, the left foot, into the reflection, noting its quietness and thanking God for creating it. I slowly move up past my feet and focus on the solitude of the shin. I continue moving slowly up my body, noting at each stage how peaceful and content each body part is and thanking God for it. I do this exercise very slowly, spending a while at each spot without becoming stuck on any one.

When I have reached the top of my head, I pull away slowly and try to get a sense of my entire body as a "unified whole" at rest and at peace. I go back "into my body" very slowly, traveling through my various body parts, again observing the stillness that pervades everywhere. I now pull away again and revisit the quietness of my entire body.

I spend a few minutes soaking in that quiet state.

RELATED ENTRIES

Awe, Hate, Jealous, Lonely, Sad, Sexually Aroused

WORDS TO TAKE WITH YOU

Blessed are You, Adonai, Ruler of the universe, who has
formed human beings in wisdom, and created in us a system
of ducts and tubes. It is well known before Your glorious
throne that if but one of these be opened, or if one of those
be closed, it would be impossible to exist in Your presence.
Blessed are You, Adonai, who heals all creatures and
does wonders.
—Asher Yotzar, an old Jewish prayer said
after leaving the bathroom

BODY

1/7/14

GOD, I'M TOO BUSY

Then Jesus said to him, "Someone gave a great dinner and invited many. At the time for the dinner he sent his slave to say to those who had been invited, 'Come; for everything is ready now.' But they all alike began to make excuses. The first said to him, 'I have bought a piece of land, and I must go out and see it; please accept my regrets.' Another said, 'I have bought five yoke of oxen, and I am going to try them out; please accept my regrets.'"
—Luke 14:16–19

God wills that I work hard and contribute to the progress of humanity. But God does not will for me to be too busy. If I am too busy, then I am not taking care of the body, mind and spirit that God has entrusted to me. Nor am I doing any favors to those I serve, since I am not truly giving my healthiest, holiest, happiest self. So, while there may be brief periods when I must endure an overwhelming schedule, I should not allow myself to be in a permanent state of being overwhelmed with tasks to perform. If I do find myself in such a state, I must first admit that this is the result of choices that I made. I simply bit off more than I could chew. I said "yes" to more things than I could handle. The solution would be for me to learn to say "no." If this has been a problem for a while, then I need to explore in prayer what my motivation is for hurting myself this way.

One motivation may be that I am addicted to work. Just as I could misuse alcohol, drugs and food, so, too, could I misuse God's gift of work. A second motivation may be that I simply don't love myself enough to take good care of myself. I don't see myself as the precious and fragile gift that I am.

A third motivation may be that of arrogance. It is arrogant of me to think that I must be the one to solve everyone's problems. It is humble of me to admit my limitations and my inability to be the savior of anything. A hardworking priest who was taking some time off from his busy job was stopped on the street by an alcoholic, homeless man. The man told the priest about his many serious problems and asked him for money. The priest looked at him with sincere compassion and said, "I see that you have very real and very serious problems, and I'm sorry for that. But I don't believe that I'm the one who can help you with those problems right now. All that I can do is promise to pray for you." This priest was not selfish or uncaring; he simply knew his limitations and was humble enough to admit it to himself and to the homeless man.

But you can imagine what the homeless guy thought of the priest! Which brings up a fourth motivation for not being able to say "no." Very often, I am not strong enough to take others' rejection of me. I feel guilty because someone else is angry or disappointed with me. But in order to live a happy, healthy, holy life I must accept that I will at times disappoint or anger others. There are simply no other options if I wish to care for myself in the way that God wills.

SUGGESTED SCRIPTURE PASSAGES

GENESIS 1:1–2:4: God created the heavens and the earth,
then God rested

PSALM 62: My soul rests in God alone

PSALM 131: O Lord, my soul is still

ECCLESIASTES 1:1—2:26: Vanity of vanities, all is vanity

MATTHEW 6:25–34: Consider the lilies

MATTHEW 11:28–30: Come to me, all you who are weary

MATTHEW 24:36–51: We do not know the day or the hour

MARK 6:30–33: Come away awhile

LUKE 9:57–62: Let me bury my father first

LUKE 10:38–42: Martha, Martha, you are anxious
about many things

LUKE 14:15–24: Dinner guests are too busy
to accept the invitation
LUKE 16:19–31: The rich man and Lazarus

PRAYER POINTERS

Sometimes God asks me to do overwhelmingly difficult work. At other times, I simply have taken on more work than I should have. My first task in prayer, then, is to discern whether this busyness is God's will or if it is simply my problem of overloading myself with work.

If it is God's will for me right now, then I beg God for the strength to endure. I join my sufferings to Jesus' ordeal of the Passion. In that light, I see that God is not asking of me anything that his Son did not himself endure. I see that my task is puny compared to Jesus' most difficult work. I draw strength from knowing that my God is with me and has preceded me.

If it is my problem of overburdening myself, then I must explore the roots of this problem. Why is it that I have done this to myself? Is this a pattern in my life? Am I addicted to work? Do I love myself enough to take good care of myself? Do I arrogantly see myself as the only one who can solve these problems?

I prayerfully consider if there are one or more tasks that God would like me to let go of at this time. I pray for the courage and strength it will take for me to admit to others that I simply can't handle this right now. I spiritually prepare myself for the consequences, knowing that God will be with me through it all. I pray over my calendar, evaluating each item this way.

RELATED ENTRIES

Confront, Hate, Ministry, Noontime, Stressed, Weary

WORDS TO TAKE WITH YOU

Burnout is when your true motives come home to roost.
—Anonymous

The mark of the immature man is that he wants to die
nobly for a cause, while the mark of the mature man is that he
wants to live humbly for one.
—Wilhelm Stekel, quoted in *The Catcher in the Rye*
by J. D. Salinger

BUSY

GOD, I'M AFRAID OF CHANGE

> For surely I know the plans I have for you, says the LORD, plans for your welfare and not for harm, to give you a future with hope. Then when you call upon me and come and pray to me, I will hear you. When you search for me, you will find me; if you seek me with all your heart, I will let you find me, says the LORD, and I will restore your fortunes and gather you from all the nations and all the places where I have driven you, says the LORD, and I will bring you back to the place from which I sent you into exile.
> —Jeremiah 29:11–14

Years ago, during a particularly difficult period of transition, I found myself praying the rosary a bit more than usual. In the midst of it one day, I realized why it was such a comfort to me. I prayed the rosary while trying to adjust to a new assignment because the rosary brought me back home. It brought me back to the place I felt most stable and secure: my childhood. My memories of praying the rosary with my family are almost palpable. I remember all of us kneeling on the wooden floor of the living room of our small wood-frame house on West Keller Street. I remember the tiny candlelight and the darkness surrounding it. I remember the feel of the rosary beads between my fingers and the sound of the cadences of Hail Marys, Our Fathers and Glory Be to the Fathers. I returned to the rosary during that time of transition because the rosary, and all those other Catholic rituals, were an important link between my past and present.

There is a quiet little gesture that the priest performs in the middle of the Mass that many Catholics probably don't always notice. Just after the Lamb of God, the priest breaks a tiny piece of the host and drops it into the chalice. Legend has it that this ritual goes all the way back to the early church. Before there were priests, only bishops could consecrate the bread and wine. But before long there were so many Christians in the city that they could not handle all the crowds, so the new office of the priesthood was established. In the beginning the people were afraid of change—they did not believe that a priest had the authority to consecrate. So young men stood by during the bishop's Mass, and just after the consecration, the bishop handed each of them a small piece of the host. They ran all through the city dropping the small pieces into the chalices of the priests' Masses. This symbolic gesture taught the people that there is only one Sacrifice of the Mass in which we all participate. We still do this liturgical gesture today to remind us of the same lesson. It reminds us that the Mass I celebrate in Houston is the same Mass my family is celebrating in my hometown in Louisiana. It's the same Mass my Jesuit friend is celebrating in Siberia, the same Mass as is celebrated in every place I've ever had to say good-bye to. It's the same Mass as the pope's in Rome, and it's the same Eternal Banquet that is celebrated by all my loved ones and ancestors who have gone ahead of me to heaven.

When I am going through a difficult period of change in my life, I seek the consolation of those ancient rituals that remind me of my God and Savior, who is beyond all change. On the foundation of that rock, all earthly change is manageable.

SUGGESTED SCRIPTURE PASSAGES

GENESIS 12:1–9: The call of Abraham
ISAIAH 42:1–16: Sing a new song
ISAIAH 43:16–21: Look, I am doing something new
ISAIAH 65:17–25: A new heaven and a new earth
JEREMIAH 18: The potter
JEREMIAH 29:11–14: I know the plans I have for you
MATTHEW 1:18–25: Joseph's dream

MATTHEW 7:24–27: Build your house on rock
LUKE 1:26–56: Mary's "yes"
LUKE 5:36–38: Old wine, new wineskins
LUKE 19:1–10: Come down, Zacchaeus
JOHN 20:19–20: The apostles in the upper room, hiding
ACTS 10:9–33: Peter accepts "unclean" food for the first time

PRAYER POINTERS

I reflect on Cardinal Newman's words below. I ponder the fact that I must allow change in my life if I am to continue to grow. I reflect on the ways that this particular change might help me to grow. I ask God to show me the many graces God can give me only if I say "yes" to this change.

I prayerfully look back at my past and see that the times I have accepted changes in my life have been some of the most enriching and maturing moments of my life. I trust that God will make this change a grace-filled one as well.

In prayer I try to get to the root of my fear. What is the worst-case scenario here? In the light of prayer I realize that most of my fears are unfounded. I allow my objective mind to console my frightened and irrational heart. Even for those fears that may become a reality, I prayerfully recognize that God will always be there to protect me and keep me from harm. I place that trust in God.

During periods of transition, I rely on the ancient prayers and rituals of the church to remind me that, while my life is changing, I can put my trust in the Unchanging One. God is the rock my house is built on, and that foundation will keep me strong.

RELATED ENTRIES

Afraid, Despair, Lost, Procrastinator, Worried

WORDS TO TAKE WITH YOU

To grow is to change; to be perfect is to change often.
—Cardinal Newman

Life is a bridge. Cross over it, but build no house on it.
—Indian Proverb

Unless you do something beyond what you have already
mastered, you will never grow.
—Ralph Waldo Emerson

A foolish consistency is the hobgoblin of little minds.
—Ralph Waldo Emerson

Do one thing every day that scares you.
—Baz Lermin

Custom without truth is just old error.
—Cyprian

CHANGE

GOD, I NEED TO CONFRONT SOMEONE

Do not think that I have come to bring peace to the earth;
I have not come to bring peace, but a sword.
> For I have come to set a man against his father,
> and a daughter against her mother,
> and a daughter-in-law against her mother-in-law;
> and one's foes will be members of one's own household.
—Matthew 10:34–36

As a Christian, I am called to win over hearts and minds to Christ. But I am more often called to do so with gentle cajoling than with angry confrontation. There are two major problems with confrontation. First, if I am honest with myself, I will see that my confrontation is often rooted in my own anger rather than in Christian love. Second, in the promotion of Christian values and ideals, confrontation is often an ineffective tool. It causes the person being confronted to be defensive of the status quo rather than open to new ideas or new ways of life. If, however, I couch my words in unconditional love and acceptance, then that person will feel less threatened by the challenge to change. The old adage is true: I can catch more flies with honey than with vinegar.

There are times, however, when the most loving thing to do is to openly confront someone. If I feel inclined to do so, then I must spend a lot of time in prayer, discerning whether this is truly God's will. I must thoroughly explore my motives and my plan of action.

I must also spiritually prepare myself for rejection and perhaps even hatred. Archbishop Oscar Romero, because he opposed the massacres conducted by the El Salvadoran military, knew that it was only a matter of time before he would be assassinated. Jesus had a strong sense of what was ahead for him as he prayed in the garden of Gethsemane about his inevitable crucifixion. Luke tells us, "In his anguish he prayed more earnestly, and his sweat became like great drops of blood falling down on the ground" (22:44).

In my personal experience, however (and it seems to be so in the experience of Jesus and of Romero as well), I have discovered that a certain peace can be drawn from the knowledge that I am doing my best, and that since this is the Lord's work, I can trust that the Lord will take good care of me. J. Lubbock has a very simple statement about this: "When we have done our best, we should await the result in peace."

I can't say how many times I have drawn strength from this little maxim. During the times when I feel called by God to do something unpleasant, this statement becomes a sort of mantra for me. I whisper it to my anxious heart over and over again not only in my prayer times but throughout the difficult days. I often find that the peace I draw from that mantra is contagious—that it spreads to all of the others involved. Even those on the receiving end of the confrontation or bad news seem to be affected by my demeanor of quiet serenity. Through that peace, I have found that I am better able to convey my sincere love for that person, which hopefully is the root of my unpleasant words and actions.

CONFRONT

SUGGESTED SCRIPTURE PASSAGES

EXODUS 3:4–14: God calls Moses to confront Pharaoh
2 SAMUEL 12:1–13: Nathan confronts David
PSALM 27: Though war rise up against me,
yet I will be confident
JEREMIAH 1:15–19: Jeremiah sent to confront the nations
JEREMIAH 20:7–18: I could not keep quiet
MATTHEW 7:1–5: Don't judge others
MATTHEW 18:15–20: If someone has a problem
MATTHEW 23:1–39: Jesus versus the Pharisees

MARK 8:31–33: Jesus to Peter: "Get away from me, Satan"
LUKE 2:22–35: A sword will pierce your soul
LUKE 9:44–62: The Son of Man will be betrayed
LUKE 12:1–12: When they bring you before the authorities
LUKE 12:49–59: I have not come to bring peace, but division!
LUKE 21:12–19: Dark days are coming
LUKE 22:31–34: I have prayed for you, Peter
ROMANS 8:26–39: What can separate us from the love of Christ?
GALATIANS 2:11–14: Paul publicly confronts Peter
GALATIANS 6:1–10: If someone is in sin, gently set him right
1 PETER 3:8–17: Be prepared to give an account for
the hope that is in you

PRAYER POINTERS

I use Lubbock's quote as my mantra in prayer. I pray for trust in the Lord's protection.

I pray with Jesus at the garden of Gethsemane. In my imagination, I clutch tightly Jesus' hands as we both pray about the upcoming difficulties. I thank Jesus for going through this experience first. I thank him for being present to me through it all. Knowing full well the price I may have to pay, I thank God for allowing me to take up my own cross and to play a role in God's plan of salvation.

I reflect on similar troubled days in my past. I notice that when I was *not* at peace, when I was consumed with worry and fear, the fear and worry were far worse than anything that actually occurred. In other words, the negative consequences that actually came were not nearly so bad as the nightmarish things I had envisioned. So now, as I face more storms ahead, I draw strength from knowing that the Lord has counted every hair on my head and will not allow these circumstances to destroy me.

I reflect on the gifts that the Lord is giving me throughout these troubled days. I reflect on how the Lord might use these difficult times to teach me, to mature me, to strengthen me, to transform me, to humble me and so on.

I reflect on the fact that only God lasts forever; everything else is temporary. I use the old saying, "This, too, shall pass," as my mantra in my prayer and throughout the day.

RELATED ENTRIES

Afraid, Angry, Blew Up, Change, Family, Judgmental, Procrastinator

WORDS TO TAKE WITH YOU

When we have done our best,
we should await the result in peace.
—J. Lubbock

Do nothing without deliberation, but when you have acted,
do not regret it.
—Sirach 32:19

Sometimes the majority only means that all the fools
are on the same side.
—Anonymous

A position that has no martyrs in any sense of the
word is probably not important or not true.
—Sandra Schneiders

CONFRONT

GOD, I FEEL PERFECTLY CONTENT

> God saw everything that he had made, and indeed, it was
> very good.
> —Genesis 1:31

One of my all-time favorite poems is William Carlos Williams'
"The Red Wheelbarrow":

> so much depends
> upon
>
> a red wheel
> barrow
>
> glazed with rain
> water
>
> beside the white
> chickens

My high school students in Houston had no idea why I would
like such an odd little poem. This was my attempt at an expla-
nation:

Not very often, but every now and then, a person gets a
moment of epiphany, a moment when every little tiny thing in
the world seems just right and nothing, nothing seems out of
place. The thing about those moments is that they usually occur
at the most ordinary times. Reading this poem, I imagine
Williams sitting on a porch somewhere in the country with a
cup of coffee, a pencil and a blank sheet of paper beside him.
In my imagination Williams has had writer's block for several
days and is frustrated and angry about his complete lack of cre-
ativity. Then all of a sudden, for just a moment, while looking
across the yard at the wheelbarrow and the chickens, he felt
completely and utterly happy. The moment passed—but nothing was ever the same again.

Years ago, during the time I was teaching high school in Dallas, I wrote the following in my prayer journal:

> I woke up on Saturday, showered, dressed and was pouring a cup of coffee in my travel mug, preparing to drive to a wrestling meet when the thought came to me, "I could do this for a long, long time." The "this" in that statement was not only high school teaching but also Dallas, this community, this wrestling chaplaincy, this coffee mug—everything.

Although that moment occurred over eight years ago, I still remember every detail of it. I remember the grogginess in my head, the smell of the strong New Orleans coffee, the comforting feel of the twenty-year-old "Jesuit" sweatshirt I was wearing. And, like Williams, I remember feeling completely happy.

A few years later I had to leave high school teaching for four years of graduate school in Boston. But throughout this time, I kept remembering that moment with the sweatshirt and the coffee mug. And when asked by my superiors what I might like to do after grad school, my answer came easily. "I'd like to go back to high school work," I said. And today, here I am, plowing through American Literature with all of you. And I am perfectly happy. And it was all because of that moment.

> so much depends
> upon
> the weather-beaten
> sweatshirt
> beside the white plastic
> coffee mug

SUGGESTED SCRIPTURE PASSAGES

GENESIS 1–2: The creation stories

JOB 42:10–17: The Lord restores Job's prosperity

PSALM 116: What return shall I make for the good
he has done for me?
DANIEL 3:52–90: All things bless the Lord
MATTHEW 5:1–12: The beatitudes
MATTHEW 6:25–34: Consider the lilies
LUKE 10:38–42: Martha, Martha, you are anxious
about many things
PHILIPPIANS 4:4–13: I have learned to cope
in every circumstance

PRAYER POINTERS

Ignatius speaks of an experience he calls "consolation without previous cause." He says that at times God will grant me the experience of complete peace and contentedness. By "without previous cause" he means that this peace and joy may come despite the fact that there are still many problems in my life and despite the fact that nothing extraordinarily wonderful is going on at the time. Despite all of this, I feel cockeyed with joy! Ignatius says that this is one of the most grace-filled experiences one will have in this life and that one should not analyze or scrutinize it, but rather one should simply bask in its warmth and comfort. In my prayer then, I should not try to figure out why it is that I'm so happy right now. Instead, I simply sing God's praises and enjoy the gift of happiness.

I should take advantage of this joyous moment by responding in generosity to God's goodness. I ask myself, "What return shall I make for all the good that God has done for me?" I might come up with two or three concrete commitments that I reasonably can make at this time.

RELATED ENTRIES

Awe, Evening, Grateful, Joyful, Proud, Quiet

WORDS TO TAKE WITH YOU

Fear less, hope more, eat less, chew more, whine less,
breathe more, talk less, say more, hate less, love more,
and all good things will be yours.
—Swedish Proverb

God is the great humorist. It's just that
He has a slow audience to work with.
—Garrison Keillor

CONTENT

GOD, PLEASE HELP ME TO DECIDE

For thus said the Lord GOD, the Holy One of Israel:
In returning and rest you shall be saved;
    in quietness and in trust shall be your strength....

He will surely be gracious to you at the sound of your cry; when he hears it, he will answer you. Though the Lord may give you the bread of adversity and the water of affliction, yet your Teacher will not hide himself any more, but your eyes shall see your Teacher. And when you turn to the right or when you turn to the left, your ears shall hear a word behind you, saying, "This is the way; walk in it."
—Isaiah 30:15, 19–21

To use prayer as a way of helping me to decide something is called discernment. Here are some helpful tips about discernment from my favorite saint, Ignatius Loyola:

When in desolation, I should not make any big decisions. When I am depressed or in a foul mood, my objectivity goes out the window. Therefore, it is better for me to stick with prior commitments until I feel better.

I should pray for Ignatian indifference. "Ignatian indifference" refers to a state of mind wherein I am completely open to doing whatever God wants me to do. I need to pray for this grace before I begin to make my decision. Otherwise, I'll really be justifying my own wishes by saying, "I prayed about it."

At the beginning of the discernment, I must remember the end for which I am striving. I should write out a personal mission statement at the beginning of the discernment process so that I don't confuse the end with the various means to that end.

The option that looks holier may not actually be holier. Jesus says that the devil comes as a wolf in sheep's clothing. For example, the evil spirit may convince a battered wife that it is God's will to stay with this dangerous man.

The spirit of peace is usually a sign of God's will. In prayer I should imagine each of my options played out. Then I should observe which option brings me more peace when I dream about it. That peace may be God's way of telling me to go in that direction.

At the end of my life, which way would I like to look back upon? In prayer I should imagine myself on my deathbed or up in heaven playing the videotape of my life in front of God. What would I want God to see on that tape?

Once I think I have my answer, I should await confirmation from God. Even after I've come to a decision, I should place that decision before God several times, asking him to confirm that it is the right one.

I need a spiritual guide. I should keep sharing my discernment process with a wise and holy person. Ignatius says that the devil likes for me to keep secrets.

Once the process is over, I should boldly act according to the fruits of my discernment. I should turn over this decision to God and not let the future frighten me.

SUGGESTED SCRIPTURE PASSAGES

DEUTERONOMY 30:11–20: I have set before you life and death—
choose life
1 KINGS 3:1–15: Give me wisdom to judge right from wrong
WISDOM 9:1–11: Give me wisdom that sits by your throne
SIRACH 14:20–27: Happy the one who meditates on wisdom
ISAIAH 30:15–21: By waiting you shall be told,
"This is the way; walk in it."

JEREMIAH 29:11–14: I know well the plans I have for you,
plans of fullness
JEREMIAH 31:31–34: Deep within I will write my law
MATTHEW 7: On prayer and discernment
MARK 10:46–52: The blind man Bartimaeus: "I want to see!"
EPHESIANS 5:8–21: Try to discern the will of the Lord
1 JOHN 4: Test the spirits to see whether they are from God

PRAYER POINTERS

Before praying about my options, I ask God to give me the grace of Ignatian indifference, a state of being wherein I am completely open to whatever it is God wants of me. If I am in that state, I allow myself some time to feel the power and the freedom of this grace.

In prayer I write out a personal mission statement. I ask myself, "What is the end for which I strive?" I spend some time on this, knowing that until I'm clear about this, I will be tempted to confuse the end with the various means.

In my prayerful imagination, I play out my life as it would go if I chose Option A; then I play out my life as if I chose Option B, and so on. While playing these options out, I observe which one brings peace in my heart. Saint Ignatius Loyola says that this is usually the clearest sign of God's will.

Once I think I've arrived at an answer, I spend *more* time in prayer asking God for confirmation of that choice. In other words, I ask God to let me know somehow that this choice, indeed, is God's will.

Once I have come to my decision, I don't look back. I turn it over to God, knowing that the Lord will make good come from the situation regardless of my actions. I trust that he will do so.

RELATED ENTRIES

Change, Lost, Procrastinator

WORDS TO TAKE WITH YOU

Man is created to praise, reverence and serve God our Lord, and by this means to save his soul....Consequently, as far as we are concerned, we should not prefer health to sickness, riches to poverty, honor to dishonor, a long life to a short life....Our one desire and choice should be what is more conducive to the end for which we are created.
—First Principle and Foundation, Saint Ignatius Loyola

You thought, as a boy, that a mage is one who can do anything. So I thought once. So did we all. And the truth is that as a man's real power grows and his knowledge widens, ever the way he can follow grows narrower until at last he chooses nothing, but does only and wholly what he *must* do.
—Ogion the Wizard in *A Wizard of Earthsea* by Ursula LeGuin

The heart has its reasons which reason knows not of.
—Blaise Pascal

The freer we are, the fewer choices we have.
—John O'Donnell, S.J.

The finest bread is as poison to the one who is not called to eat it, and the most deadly poison is as the finest bread to the one who is called to consume it.
—Pierre Causade (paraphrased)

DECIDE

GOD, I'M IN DESPAIR

When he reached the place, he said to them, "Pray that you may not come into the time of trial." Then he withdrew from them about a stone's throw, knelt down, and prayed, "Father, if you are willing, remove this cup from me; yet, not my will but yours be done." Then an angel from heaven appeared to him and gave him strength. In his anguish he prayed more earnestly, and his sweat became like great drops of blood falling down on the ground.
—Luke 22:40–44

So, I'm on my annual eight-day retreat, and I'm hiking through the woods in northern New Mexico. I get to the top of a high peak and notice some caves there. I plan to explore them, but first I sit on a ledge and enjoy the panoramic view. While lazily looking at the woods below me, I see in the distance a black fur ball go by. "That couldn't be…could it?" I had heard lots of stories of bears in these parts—some of them were not pleasant stories. I sit there trying to convince myself that it couldn't possibly be what I thought it was, but to no avail. I suddenly have a change of heart about visiting those caves and instead want badly to be back home.

I start my descent, nervously realizing that I will have to go in the vicinity of the fur ball sighting. Sure enough, about halfway down, what should jump out of the woods and right onto my path about thirty yards from me but a big black bear! I had been told by the locals that one of the best ways of dealing with bears in the wild was to make myself as big as possible and to yell and scream in hopes that, at the very least, the bear would find me more trouble than it's worth and go away. So, standing as tall as I could and lifting my puny walking stick high in the air, I let out a yell. But this was no ordinary yell. What was released from my mouth was a roar I had not thought possible for any human being, much less me. I roared and roared and roared. Believe it or not, the bear jumped with fear (honest!) and dove into the brush. I knew that my troubles were not necessarily over though because the bear was ahead of me on the trail and there was simply no other way of getting down. Step by shaky step I descended, and sure enough, as I turned another corner, there was my big buddy, this time sitting on the trail, apparently waiting for me. Once again I emitted a sound I thought only apes could make. Once again the bear jumped back into the woods, but this time—I must admit—he looked more curious (amused?) than frightened! Thankfully that was my last sighting, and I made it back home safely.

Later, sitting on the back porch and drinking my second Corona, I laughed and asked God why on earth he would send me a bear on my retreat. What was he trying to tell me? God laughed, too. But then, in my imagination, God got serious and said something I'll never forget as long as I live. Reminding me of my unheard of and unbelievable yell, God said to me, "You see, I have hidden resources inside you that you cannot even fathom. Remember that the next time you face a seemingly insurmountable problem."

SUGGESTED SCRIPTURE PASSAGES

JOB 3:1–4: Curse the day of my birth
WISDOM 3.1–9: The souls of the just are in the hand of God
MARK 5:21–43: A woman is healed; a dead girl is raised
MARK 15:33–34: My God, why have you forsaken me?
LUKE 22—23: Luke's Passion narrative
LUKE 22:40–46: Jesus sweats blood in the garden of Gethsemane
JOHN 11:1–44: Martha and Mary's grief over Lazarus
1 CORINTHIANS 1:4–9: You lack no spiritual gift

PRAYER POINTERS

In prayer I go back through the past, remembering other times in my life when I thought I had reached an insurmountable problem. I remember how distressed I felt then. At the time it seemed as though I would not survive, and yet here I am today looking back at what is now just a distant memory. I allow Jesus to console me now, telling me that we will get through this— that one day this seemingly fatal moment will also be only a memory. If I feel called to do so, I place my problems and fears back into the hands of God and renew my trust in his divine providence.

I pray over Jesus' agony in the garden of Gethsemane. In my imagination I kneel next to Jesus in his moment of despair. I see the tears and sweat dripping from his face and realize that he is as terrified and distressed as I feel right now. I allow this distraught Jesus to tell me about his anguish. I thank and praise Jesus for choosing to go through such a terrible ordeal for me. I try to console Jesus and let him know that he is going to be OK, that things will get very bad but that he will resurrect in the end. I then allow Jesus to look me in the eyes and tell me the exact same thing.

I read 1 Corinthians 1:4–9. I allow God to show me the abundant resources that he has hidden inside me. One by one, I name each of the gifts that God has given me until I come to the profound realization that, as Saint Paul says, I lack nothing that I need. God has provided me with every essential gift needed to get through this time of crisis.

RELATED ENTRIES

Addicted, Change, Confront, Doubts, Lost, Nighttime,
Stressed, Worried

DESPAIR

WORDS TO TAKE WITH YOU

Everything can be taken from a man but one thing: the last of
the human freedoms—to choose one's attitude in any given
set of circumstances, to choose one's own way.
—Viktor Frankl

DESPAIR

GOD, I HAVE DOUBTS

> Someone from the crowd answered him, "Teacher, I brought you my son; he has a spirit that makes him unable to speak; and whenever it seizes him, it dashes him down; and he foams and grinds his teeth and becomes rigid; and I asked your disciples to cast it out, but they could not do so.... It has often cast him into the fire and into the water, to destroy him; but if you are able to do anything, have pity on us and help us." Jesus said to him, "If you are able!—All things can be done for the one who believes." Immediately the father of the child cried out, "I believe; help my unbelief!"
> —Mark 9:17–18, 22–24

An atheist was walking along a cliff one day when he suddenly slipped and fell. Halfway down, he was able to grab a weak little branch. Hanging there and knowing that the branch wouldn't hold him forever, the guy looked up into the sky and yelled, "OK, if there's anybody up there, save me now, and I'll believe in you." With great tenderness God spoke to the man, "My son, I will save you. Let go of the branch." The man thought about it a minute, looked down into the deep ravine and then back up into the heavens and yelled, "Is there anybody else up there?"

When I was a kid, my teenaged brother, Greg, would sometimes interrupt my all-important TV watching with "Come on. I need you to help me start the truck." I begrudgingly went outside and found my place in the lineup between other brothers and/or neighbors at the back of Greg's 1969 Ford pickup. The bunch of us would push it as fast as possible down our quiet little street while Greg kept turning the ignition and pumping the gas. Eventually, the little truck would remember how to do this on its own, and off he went.

This little trick of getting a running start has proven useful in other areas of life. If I lose my train of thought while giving a speech, I can often just keep talking a minute or two and my brain will "kick in" again. If I get stuck during my writing, I just keep going, writing gibberish if I have to. Eventually, my fingers will find the right keys again. I have a feeling this little trick works for big stuff, too. I'll bet married people use this trick to get through the rough spots. They just keep going in the direction they're supposed to go until it feels right and natural again.

Saint Ignatius Loyola advises that if I'm having problems believing or if I know in my head the right thing to do but my heart is resisting, then I should act *as if* I do believe, *as if* my heart were fully amenable until I do, in fact, believe again with my whole heart and soul. Oftentimes, when my faith wavers, I take great consolation in this advice. First, it reminds me that doubting is a common phenomenon and not necessarily a sin. Second, it tells me what I should do while waiting for my feeble faith to return. I act *as if.* I go through the motions, not as a hypocrite but as one who has allowed his *will* to push him through when his heart is acting fickle. This is why the church values ritual so much. It allows my body and my voice to move me through the barren deserts of my spiritual life. Eventually, my heart and soul will kick in again. I just have to be patient.

And from pushing my brother's truck, I've learned also that I might need to grab some friends and family to help push me down the road a bit until I can do it on my own again.

DOUBTS

SUGGESTED SCRIPTURE PASSAGES

GENESIS 18:1–15: Sarah laughs, doubting God's promise
MATTHEW 17:14–21: If you had the faith of a mustard seed
MARK 5:21–42: Jesus heals a woman and raises a dead girl
MARK 9:14–29: I do believe; help my unbelief
JOHN 20:19–29: Doubting Thomas
1 CORINTHIANS 1:18–25: Jews demand signs
and Greeks look for wisdom
1 CORINTHIANS 2:6–16: Eyes have not seen; ears have not heard

HEBREWS 11:1–3: Faith is the assurance of things hoped for

JAMES 1:2–7: The testing of your faith produces endurance

PRAYER POINTERS

In most cases doubting is not a sin, since it usually wells up without my choosing it. When I have doubts it is important to face them honestly rather than pretend they don't exist. Most importantly, I need to bring those doubts to God. I need to tell God that my faith in him is not so strong. Since Saint Ignatius insists that we always tell God what we need, I must tell God that I need to feel his presence or witness his action in the world in a more concrete way. If I need to, I'll even shake my fist at him as Job, Jonah and many others did. I may chide him for abandoning me as Jesus did. I know in my head, of course, that God never abandons me, but in my heart I'm feeling this way and I must let God know that.

When my soul is faltering, I allow my body and my will to do the heavy lifting. I turn to more ritualistic prayers. I tell God that my body will have to pray for me (through kneeling and standing at Mass, for example) while my heart and soul are wavering.

In prayer I come up with a few people to whom I can go with this problem. I need loved ones to carry me through this time. In Mark 5:25–34 the hemorrhaging woman was healed merely through touching the tassel of Jesus. Spiritual writer Ronald Rolheiser says that when my faith is weak, the faith of loved ones can be that tassel of Christ, touching and healing me vicariously.

RELATED ENTRIES

Despair, Dry, Lost, Marriage

WORDS TO TAKE WITH YOU

Human beings cannot receive answers to questions
they have never asked.
—Paul Tillich

There's a good bit of agnostic in all of us.
None of us knows much—only enough to trust
to reach out a hand into the dark.
—Margaret Craven, *I Heard the Owl Call My Name*

DOUBTS

GOD, I'M SPIRITUALLY DRY

O, that you would tear open the heavens and come down,
    so that the mountains would quake at your presence—
...
When you did awesome deeds that we did not expect,
    you came down, the mountains quaked at your presence.
From ages past no one has heard,
    no ear has perceived,
no eye has seen any God besides you,
    who works for those who wait for him.
...
We have all become like one who is unclean,
    and all our righteous deeds are like a filthy cloth.
We all fade like a leaf,
    and our iniquities, like the wind, take us away.
—Isaiah 64:1, 3–4, 6–7

Many people have the mistaken notion that those who have a strong prayer life never have problems experiencing God's presence in prayer. But any long-term pray-er will tell you that it is not unusual to go through long periods without feeling anything at all in one's prayer. Thérèse of Lisieux, John of the Cross, Ignatius Loyola, Teresa of Avila—all of the great mystics of the church have spoken of the common experience of dryness in one's spiritual life. Mystics of our day have said the same. Henri Nouwen, one of the most important spiritual writers of our time, once said, "[My prayer time is not a time]...of deep prayer, nor a time in which I experience a special closeness to God; it is not a period of serious attentiveness to the divine mysteries. I wish it were! On the contrary, it is full of distractions, inner restlessness, sleepiness, confusion, and boredom. It seldom, if ever, pleases my senses." And Mother Teresa of Calcutta, not long before her death, was asked, "How does it feel to be so close to God?" She answered, "It's been so long since I've felt close to God that I don't remember what it feels like." One who is spiritually dry should take comfort from such auspicious company. While our faith tells us that God is always present, the experience of the church tells us that, for whatever reason, God sometimes allows us to go through periods in which we do not *feel* his presence.

Sometimes it's even worse than that: sometimes we don't even feel the *desire* to feel God's presence. This experience can embarrass us, and we often deny it. I remember once going through such a period in my spiritual life. My spiritual director sensed it and asked, "Mark, do you desire to be closer to God right now?" I nervously said, "Well, of course I do!" and chattered away about some pious notion that was unrelated to the topic. The director let me talk a moment and then asked again, "Mark, do you desire to be closer to God?" Again I deflected the question. But the third time she asked, my shoulders slumped and I fell back into the chair, defeated. Staring up at the ceiling, I confessed, "No. Right now, I don't even *want* to be with God." She smiled and said, "Now we're getting somewhere!" We spent the rest of the conversation talking about what to do with this mood. She reminded me of Saint Ignatius's advice, that when I don't feel God's presence, I need to pray at least for the desire of God's presence. With great compassion, Ignatius advised further that if I can't even do that, then perhaps I could pray for *the desire for the desire*. Now that's a prayer I can always handle.

SUGGESTED SCRIPTURE PASSAGES

JUDITH 8:25–27: Not for vengeance did the Lord test them
JOB 6—7: Job is angry with God
PSALM 22: My God, why have you forsaken me?
PSALM 63:1–9: All through the night I will meditate on you
PSALM 77: Will God spurn us forever,
and never again be favorable?
PSALM 102: I am withered, dried up like the grass

PSALM 143:6–7: My soul thirsts for you
ISAIAH 43:14–21: See, I am doing something new
ISAIAH 63:15–19: Look down from heaven, O Lord
ISAIAH 64: O, that you would tear open the heavens
and come down!
MATTHEW 7:7–11: Seek and you shall find
MARK 4:35–41: Jesus sleeping in the boat
MARK 15:33–34: My God, why have you forsaken me?
LUKE 11:5–13: If one keeps knocking, the master arises
JAMES 5:7–11: Wait for Christ's coming

PRAYER POINTERS

While waiting for my prayer life to pick up, I can always go back to easier forms of prayer that do not require me to focus as well. I can pray the rosary, the Liturgy of the Hours or I can use some ready-made prayer book that has worked for me in the past.

I prayerfully evaluate the logistics of my prayer times. Do I pray at a bad time of day? Do I use the best prayer posture (that is, a position that is relaxed and yet keeps me awake)? Am I giving myself enough time to pray? Have I done what I could to rid myself of distractions? Do I seek the advice of a spiritual director or mentor?

I prayerfully ask myself if there is some unacknowledged problem between God and me. Am I angry with God about something? Do I have a fear that I have not yet faced?

I prayerfully return to a time when prayer was going well. What was I praying about then? What Bible passage was I using? What prayer approach? I return to whatever it was that worked back then.

I look back through the past day and ask myself: where was God present to me? Who wore God's face today? I prayerfully return to that moment of my day and praise God for it. I consider how I might respond to such love.

As always, it is important that I tell God what I desire. If I desire to feel his presence, I must prayerfully beg God to give me such an experience. If I don't even have that desire, then I should pray for that desire to come to me.

I slowly read Mark 4:35–41. In my imagination I notice that, though the boat ride is rough because of the ensuing storm, Jesus is so tired that he just can't keep his eyes open anymore. So I go over to him and say, "It's OK, Lord. I will sit by your side as you sleep." I make that statement my mantra, repeating it over and over again. I try to imagine myself sitting by the side of Jesus as he sleeps. Though my spiritual storm grows more furious, I am not concerned. Instead, I look with love on my friend and Lord, keeping still so as not to wake him.

At the end of my prayer time, I tell God how I'm feeling about our relationship at this time. I let him know if I feel frustrated, angry, confused and so on. As best I can, I close with a prayer of surrender, something like this: "God, I don't understand why you're allowing me to feel distant from you right now, but I trust that you will always do what is best for me. So I place my prayer life in your hands, and I accept whatever it is you wish to do with it. If you call me into the desert, I willingly accept your call. Give me the strength to follow through."

RELATED ENTRIES

Angry at You, Doubts, Lonely, Lost, Quiet

WORDS TO TAKE WITH YOU

Only those who walk in the dark see the stars.
—Anonymous

That which you are seeking is causing you to seek.
—Buddha

Jesus will return when we want Him enough.
—Teilhard de Chardin, s.j.

Jesus says, "You would not search for me if I had not already found you."
—Anonymous

"Does the Keeper ever speak to you, Uss-Uss?"
"In the thrumming of the roots of trees under the earth, she speaks to me," said Uss-Uss.
"What does she say?"
"Unfortunately, I don't speak the language of trees," said Uss-Uss. "I haven't the faintest idea."
—Orson Scott Card

GOD, SOMEONE I LOVE IS DYING

As for me, I feel that the last drops of my life are being poured out for God. The time for my departure has arrived. The glorious fight that God gave me I have fought, the course that I was set I have finished, and I have kept the faith. The future for me holds the crown of righteousness which the Lord, the true judge, will give to me in that day.

—2 Timothy 4:6–8 (Modern English translation)

As a deacon, only months before my priestly ordination, my Jesuit priest friend and mentor, Father Harry Tompson, passed away. Here are some snippets of my reflections from my last week with him.

...The heavy medication had Harry feeling agitated and unable to sit still. He kept trying to focus on one thing or another, but could not sustain a logical string of thoughts. He began, "Mark you've got to fix the...the..." and he lay there moving his index finger backward and forward as though gently trying to jump-start his mind again. Trying to be helpful I said, "The car, Harry?" "Yes," he said, "...you've got to take my car and... [a long pause while Harry shut his eyes tight in concentration]... take the keys that are there in my... in my..." Finally, he gave up, looked at me and repeated something he'd said many times that week, "Don't die, Mark. It's no picnic." Then he turned his head away.

After a minute or two, I said, "Harry, how about you lay back quietly while I read the Breviary aloud to you." Like a drowning man grasping for rope, his eyes grew wide and he said, "OK." Then he lay down, closed his eyes and listened as I read the words:

> I remember the days that are past:
> I ponder all your works.
> I muse on what your hand has wrought
> And to you I stretch out my hands.
> Like a parched land my soul thirsts for you.

While reading the lines, my voice grew more and more shaky. Though I was sick with grief, there was something that felt so right about that moment. I remember thinking to myself, "This is what it's supposed to be like: the young deacon reciting the words of the Breviary for his dying pastor and mentor. This is the kind of life and death I've wanted for myself. It's what I prayed for as a novice."

I kept trying to turn off my emotions as I read. I knew that Harry needed me to be strong just then, so I kept choking back the tears and read on:

> Lord, make haste and answer;
> For my spirit fails within me.
> Do not hide your face
> Lest I become like those in the grave.

My efforts failed. I had to stop reading because my crying was taking over. I was angry with myself for ruining this important moment for Harry, but then I looked back at him and noticed that he had fallen into a peaceful sleep.

SUGGESTED SCRIPTURE PASSAGES

DEUTERONOMY 34: When Moses dies
1 KINGS 2:1–11: When David dies
2 KINGS 2:1–15: Elijah in the whirlwind
PSALM 23: Though I walk through the shadow of death

ISAIAH 35:1–10: A song of hope
ISAIAH 40:1–11: Every valley shall be lifted up;
every hill will be made low
LUKE 11:5–13: Ask and you shall receive;
knock and it shall be opened
LUKE 22:39–46: Father, if it is your will, take this cup from me
LUKE 23:26–31: Weeping women
LUKE 23:44–49: The death of Jesus
JOHN 6:22–58: I am the bread of life
JOHN 10:11–18: I am the good shepherd
JOHN 11:1–44: Lazarus's death
JOHN 14:1–3: In my Father's house
there are many dwelling places
ROMANS 8: Sufferings of the present are nothing
compared to glory
2 CORINTHIANS 4:1—5:10: We carry in our bodies
the dying of Jesus
COLOSSIANS 1:22–29: In my flesh I fill up
what is lacking in the sufferings of Christ
2 TIMOTHY 4:6–8: I have run the good race…
my crown awaits
1 PETER 1:3–9: You may have to suffer for a time

PRAYER POINTERS

I may find any sort of meditation, contemplation or prayer that requires concentration and stillness too difficult right now. My situation may be simply too emotionally tumultuous for me to settle myself. In that case, I may find ready-made prayer (for example: the rosary, written prayers from a prayer book, or the Liturgy of the Hours) more helpful. This type of prayer requires little concentration on my part, so if my mind or emotions begin to wander, the prayers themselves will take me back.

DYING

If prayer is difficult for the loved ones of the dying, it is often even more so in the experience of the dying persons themselves. Many prayerful people expect to have powerful experiences in prayer near the end of their lives and are disappointed when, because of medication or other factors, they can hardly pray at all. If I feel called to it, I might want to ask my dying friend if she wants to pray together. Very often, even not so religious people long to pray but are too bashful or afraid to ask for help. If she is interested, I could pray simple prayers such as the Lord's Prayer or the Hail Mary. She may be able to pray aloud with me, but even if she can't, she could mentally follow along. Within myself, I often feel humbled and grateful for the privilege of praying in place of someone unable to do so. If she really enjoys praying together, I may want to establish some sort of ritual, such as praying the rosary with her every night before she sleeps.

Perhaps my most important prayer at this time is simply the prayer of silent presence. That is, the long periods of time I sit quietly by her bedside while she sleeps or rests. In my own experience, I have found this to be a profound experience of prayer. I can sense God's presence in the room as I lovingly wait by the bedside. Often at these times I am struck with awe at the wonder of God's gift of life, and I might even have the gift of gratitude for the whole cycle of life, death and resurrection to which we are all called.

RELATED ENTRIES

Afraid, Angry at You, Change, Grieving, Nighttime, Sad

WORDS TO TAKE WITH YOU

Now that I have found the joy of utilizing all forms of growth to make you, or to let you, grow in me, grant that I may willingly consent to this last phase of communion in the course of which I shall possess you by diminishing in you. When the signs of age begin to mark my body (and still more when they touch my mind); when the ill that is to diminish me or carry me off strikes from without or is born within me; when the painful moment comes in which I suddenly awaken to the fact that I am ill or growing old; and above all at that last moment when I feel I am losing hold of myself and am absolutely passive within the hands of the great unknown forces that have formed me; in all those dark moments, O God, grant that I may understand that it is you (provided only my faith is strong enough) who are painfully parting the fibers of my being in order to penetrate to the very marrow of my substance and bear me away within yourself.

—"Prayer of a dying man," Teilhard de Chardin, S.J.

To live is to suffer; to survive is to find meaning in the suffering. If there is a purpose in life at all, there must be a purpose in suffering and in dying.

—Gordon Allport

Showing up is mostly everything.

—Gregory Boyle, S.J.

Death is not extinguishing the light. It is putting out the lamp because the dawn has come.

—Tagore

Tragic moments are opportunities for heroism.

—Anonymous

DYING

GOD, IT'S EVENING

The apostles gathered around Jesus, and told him all that they had done and taught. He said to them, "Come away to a deserted place all by yourselves and rest a while." For many were coming and going, and they had no leisure even to eat. And they went away in the boat to a deserted place by themselves.
—Mark 6:30–32

I really love the scene from the Bible passage above. Earlier, Jesus had sent the apostles off on their first mission by themselves. And things went well, very well. The apostles have returned, exhausted but thrilled with all of the wonders God worked through them. They can't contain their joy, and all of them are talking at the same time as they tell Jesus all about their adventures. Jesus is smiling a paternal smile. He's very proud and happy. "Come by yourselves to an out-of-the-way place," he says. I can imagine the intimacy shared between them in this scene and the bond that now exists because of the accomplishment of common mission.

The story in Mark goes on to say that the people loved them so much that they ran ahead to the not-so-hidden hiding place and were waiting for the apostles when they arrived. But at the very least, Jesus and the apostles had that quiet boat ride in the sunset. I can easily picture them drifting along on the placid waters, in no hurry to get any place. Three of them have fallen asleep. Peter can't resist putting a fishing line in the water. Matthew hates being on the water and sits in the middle of the boat, nervously telling the others not to rock it too much. James and John are teasing him about this and are rocking the boat even more, which makes Jesus laugh out loud. And all the while, despite their exhaustion, they can't help telling each other stories about all the ways God worked through their hands and feet and words and actions. They are drunk on joy.

I can easily imagine this scene because I've had many similar evenings with Jesus and our mutual friends. There is no greater feeling than to "come away" to dinnertime with friends or family at the end of a long and productive day. I've sat on many a porch or patio on such an evening and allowed the cicadas and fireflies to lull me into a quieter state. Watching the sun begin to droop sleepily, it seems the whole world is peaceful and content. A friend of mine was fond of saying, "Even the hands of the clock are resting—just hanging there—at 6:30 in the evening."

And always Jesus is there, sleepily sitting next to me on the swing. Together, without even trying and sometimes not even conscious of it, we praise the Father who blessed our labor of the day and who blesses the peace and stillness of this evening.

> Sun and moon, bless the Lord...
> Stars of heaven, bless the Lord.
> —Daniel 3:62, 63 (NAB)

SUGGESTED SCRIPTURE PASSAGES

PSALM 46:9–12: Be still and know I am God
PSALM 131: O Lord, my soul is still
MATTHEW 6:25–34: Consider the lilies
MATTHEW 11:25–30: Come to me, you who are weary
MARK 6:30–33: Come away awhile
LUKE 5:15–16: Jesus would often slip away to pray
LUKE 10:17–24: The disciples return home rejoicing
LUKE 10:38–42: Martha and Mary
LUKE 12:1–12: When they bring you before the authorities
LUKE 24:13–35: Were not our hearts burning within us?

PRAYER POINTERS

I sit quietly in the evening after a long and productive day. I allow myself to relax and enjoy the stillness of the evening as images of

EVENING

the day peacefully drift by. I do not use this time to plan for tomorrow or to critique my recent actions. I just let the world drift by for a few minutes and enjoy the ride that is my life.

I imagine Jesus sitting next to me enjoying the leisurely nature of the evening. I say nothing to him and he says nothing to me. We just sit there and enjoy each other's company.

I thank God for my good—if not perfect—life.

RELATED ENTRIES

Awe, Content, Grateful, Joyful, Ministry, Proud, Still and Quiet

WORDS TO TAKE WITH YOU

It is the time wasted with your rose that makes your rose so important.
—Antoine de Saint-Exupery

Without soul, where would a man go?
—"Jack," graffiti on the wall at Robert's Bar, New Orleans

GOD, MY FAMILY IS DRIVING ME NUTS!

> When His own people heard of this, they went out to take custody of Him; for they were saying, "He has lost his senses."
> —Mark 3:21 (NASB)

There are a variety of reasons why my family (which in my case is a religious community) might be driving me nuts. One reason may be that home is the only safe place for me to go nuts. That is, I know that they will accept me even if I do fly off the handle from time to time. In many ways, I'm not allowed to "lose it" at work, in church or among friends. I may fear rejection from the people in those circles. So, I take my pent-up aggravation and anger home to the one place I know I can release it and still be loved and accepted. Meanwhile, my family members are doing the same with me.

Ideally, family members shouldn't have to have misplaced anger, irritation and frustration dumped on them. I should work toward channeling those negative feelings in more healthy ways. I should ask the Lord to help me reflect on my own attitudes and behaviors at home. Do I always leave "the emotional leftovers" for my family? In other words, do I give my best self, my highest quality time, my most thoughtful words and actions, and my most compassionate dispositions to everyone else in my life and save whatever is left over for my family? How could I be more generous to my family in terms of quality time, emotional support and presence of mind and heart? In the meantime, while I struggle to be more generous at home, I should thank God that I have a family that allows me to dump on them, and I should pray for the strength of character to create a safe place where they might dump on me as well.

Another reason for my frustration with the family might be

FAMILY

that I expect more from them than they can actually give me. A teenager, whose father had more or less abandoned him, told me once, "I've decided that I need to go out and find my own father-figures." He then proceeded to name a variety of adults in his life on whom he relies for paternal nurturing, care and support. Over the years I have come to appreciate this idea as a profound one. No matter how great are our family members, we all need to go out and find a variety of mother-figures, father-figures, brother-figures, sister-figures and even son-figures and daughter-figures. Maybe the reason my family is driving me nuts is that they couldn't possibly fill the expansive role I expect from them. Maybe, for example, even as an adult, the mothering that I need couldn't possibly be filled by one person. I may need lots of mothers in my life. If I find a variety of moms to fill the needs I have, then maybe I could accept my biological mother for who she is and not resent her for who she is not.

SUGGESTED SCRIPTURE PASSAGES

GENESIS 4:1–16: Cain and Abel
GENESIS 33:1–11: Jacob and Esau reconcile
GENESIS 45:1–15: Joseph forgives his brothers
RUTH 1:1–18: Ruth is loyal to her mother-in-law
SIRACH 3: Honor your father, that his blessing
may come upon you
MATTHEW 20:20–28: Mother pleads for James and John
MARK 9:33–37: Disciples: "Who is the greatest?"
LUKE 2:41–52: Finding the boy Jesus in the Temple
LUKE 8:19–21: Who are my brothers and sisters?
LUKE 10:38–42: Martha and Mary
JOHN 13:1–20: Jesus washes his disciples' feet
EPHESIANS 6:1–4: Children, obey your parents

PRAYER POINTERS

I explore the possibility that I may be taking out pent-up negative emotions on my family. What are those negative emotions? What am I really angry, sad or confused about? I ask God to help me figure out how to deal directly with these problems rather than taking them out on my family.

I prayerfully explore how I might spend more quality time with my family. Or if I cannot spend more time, then how might I better use the time we do have together?

If a family member has been particularly ornery lately, I ask the Lord to help me see things through the eyes of that person. What is going on in her life right now? What battles is she fighting inside of her? How might I help the situation? What things do I do that only exacerbate the problem? What grace (for example, strength, patience, hope, courage) does she need in her life right now? I pray in petition for her to receive the graces she needs.

I prayerfully explore if I might have unrealistic expectations of a particular family member. If I have certain emotional or psychological needs that cannot be met by my spouse, brother, mother, etc., how might I healthily get these needs met elsewhere? What nonbiological family members (for example, friends, coworkers, ministers and so on) might I rely on for help in these areas of need?

I ask the Lord to show me ways I might be more generous toward members of my family, particularly the ones that are driving me crazy right now. Without compromising my integrity, how might I give my spouse the upper hand in the argument?

I prayerfully place before me in my mind each member of my family, asking God to show me his face in each of them.

RELATED ENTRIES

Angry, Confront, Forgive, Hurt, Judgmental, Marriage,
Parenting

WORDS TO TAKE WITH YOU

This house is for the ingathering of nature and human
nature. It is a house of friendships, a haven in trouble, an
open room for the encouragement of our struggle. It is a
house of freedom, guarding the dignity and worth of every
person. It offers a platform for the free voice, for declaring,
both in times of security and danger, the full and undivided
conflict of opinion. It is a house of truth-seeking, where
scientists can encourage devotion to their quest, where mystics
can abide in a community of searchers. It is a house of art,
adorning its celebrations with melodies and handiworks. It is a
house of prophecy, outrunning times past and times present
in visions of growth and progress.... This house is a cradle for
our dreams, the workshop of our common endeavor.
—Kenneth L. Patton, "This House"

After the ecstasy, go do the laundry.
—Chinese proverb

GOD, I JUST CAN'T FORGIVE

Then Peter came and said to him, "Lord, if another member of the church sins against me, how often should I forgive? As many as seven times?" Jesus said to him, "Not seven times, but, I tell you, seventy-seven times.
—Matthew 18:21–22

There are two types of forgiveness: forgiveness of the will and forgiveness of the heart. Forgiveness of the will is the choice to do all in my power, regardless of how I feel, to preserve and enhance the well-being of my offender. The all in my power part is important. Perhaps my anger will not yet allow me even to speak to my offender. Or perhaps I have discerned that it is not God's will that I be in relationship with this person at this time (for example, a battered wife might discern that it is not God's will for her to be with her husband anymore). Insofar as it is in my power to choose to forgive, I must forgive. That is what Christ teaches me to do. The choice part of that definition is important, too. Forgiveness of the will is a conscious choice that I make based on what I believe is God's will for me.

Forgiveness of the heart is a different matter. For the most part, I cannot will to experience one emotion or another. I cannot choose to feel affection for another or not to feel anger, betrayal or hurt. It simply is not in my power to do so. No, I'm going to have to pray for and wait for that gift to come from God. My choice to forgive with my will opens me up to receive the gift of forgiveness of the heart, but the gift itself must come from God.

I remember well my greatest experience of hurt and betrayal. It took me forever to get over it! It was in my daily prayer time that the Lord gradually bestowed the gift of forgiveness in my heart. Adapting the insights from a particular style of psychological therapy called *Gestalt,* I prayed in my chair with two other chairs in front of me. I sat Jesus in one of those chairs and my offender in the other. With Jesus present, I would say anything that I wanted to my offender. I might yell at him or curse him or tell him all sorts of despicable things. But at the end of my prayer time, I allowed both of my two guests to speak to me as well. At the end of our conversation, regardless of whether my heart felt it or not, I told my offender, "You hurt me, but I forgive you and I love you." And one beautiful sunny morning, I said it and realized that there was no part of me that didn't genuinely mean it, not even my heart!

SUGGESTED SCRIPTURE PASSAGES

GENESIS 45:1–15: Joseph forgives his brothers
1 SAMUEL 24: David forgives Saul
EZEKIEL 37:1–14: God revives dry bones
JONAH 4: Jonah's anger at the Lord's forgiveness
MATTHEW 5:38–48: Do not retaliate; love your enemies
MATTHEW 7:1–5: Don't judge others
MATTHEW 18:15–20: If you have a problem with
someone
MATTHEW 18:21–35: Forgive seventy-seven times
MARK 11:23–26: Forgive anyone
LUKE 5:17–26: Jesus: "Your sins are forgiven"
LUKE 6:27–36: When someone slaps you on the one cheek
LUKE 15:11–32: The Prodigal Son
LUKE 19:1–10: Come down, Zacchaeus
LUKE 23:33–38: Forgive them Father,
for they know not what they do
LUKE 23:39–43: Jesus saves the good thief
JOHN 21:15–17: Jesus forgives Peter
EPHESIANS 4:25–32: The sun must not go down on your wrath

PRAYER POINTERS

First, I work on forgiveness as an act of the will. With God I lay down exactly what I must do and must not do in order to be loving to my offender. I pay particular attention to the ways I may lash back in a passive-aggressive manner. That is, ways that I may deviously, unconsciously and subtly jab back at the offender: a well-placed comment to mutual friends, an avoidance of mutual responsibility, a "harmless joke" about her and so on. I ask God to help me avoid these sinful actions. With each future action that I contemplate, I ask Jesus to help me discern my motives. "Am I doing this out of love or revenge?" I also look back on the previous day, evaluating each of my words and actions in the same way.

I sit in my prayer chair with two other chairs in front of me. I place Jesus in one and my offender in the other. Then, I let the sparks fly, allowing all three of us to have some say. After we've all had our say, whether I feel it yet or not, I turn to my offender and say, "You hurt me, but I forgive you, and I love you."

I reflect on a time when I was forgiven by someone. I experience in my heart what it felt like to have been given this undeserved gift. I thank God for the mercy of that person, and I pray to receive that same grace of forgiveness in my life.

RELATED ENTRIES

Angry, Confront, Family, Hurt, Judgmental, Marriage

WORDS TO TAKE WITH YOU

We are like beasts when we kill.
We are like human beings when we judge.
We are like God when we forgive.
—Anonymous

To understand all is to forgive all.
—Anthony DeMello, S.J.

GOD, I'M GRATEFUL

What may I give to the Lord for all the good things that he
has done for me? I will take the cup of salvation, and give
praise to the name of the Lord. I will make the offering of
my oath to the Lord, even before all his people.
—Psalm 116:12–14 (Basic English translation)

As I watch my students eat lunch in the high school cafeteria, I
sadly witness a great deal of waste. It would not be unusual for
a boy to pull out an apple his mother packed for him, take a
bite or two out of it, and throw the rest away. It brings to mind
a story of an American missionary moving to a poor part of
Central America. She brought an apple on the flight, but never
got around to eating it. That afternoon, while unpacking in her
new home, a neighborhood girl noticed the big beautiful apple
in her bag. The missionary realized that the little girl was fascinated by the apple, so she gave it to her. The girl reverently held
the apple in both of her hands and slowly walked out of the
room, never taking her wonder-filled eyes off her gift. The missionary presumed that the girl went off somewhere to eat it, but
she found out later that the girl took it back home, diced it, and
walked around the impoverished neighborhood, giving everyone a taste of this rare and precious gift.

Gratitude is the key to a virtuous life. Conversely, all sin boils
down to ingratitude—to an abuse or neglect of God's gifts. If I
live in gratitude for some particular gift God has given me—if I
uphold it as a sacred object to be treated with reverence—then
I will not misuse that gift. A great deal of my prayer life, then,
should be that of thanking and praising God for his many gifts.
I might even want to zero in on the gifts I have abused lately
and praise God for them especially. For example, if I am rou-
tinely hard on my spouse, this problem might be an indication
that I am not appreciating the gift he has been in my life. The
more I nurture and develop a habit of thanking God for the gift

of my husband, the less inclined I will be to abuse him with my words and actions. If my sin is overeating, then, chances are, I need to praise God for the sacred vessel of my own body. My gratitude will lead me to do all that I can to keep this great gift in mint condition.

Many times Christians slip into a Pelagian mindset wherein we believe that we have to earn our way into heaven. Fear of eternal damnation, then, becomes my motivation to live virtuously. But Jesus, through the Gospels and through church teaching, tells us that heaven is a free gift from God. We could never possibly earn such a gift—it must come free of charge. If we have truly accepted this unearned salvation, then we live our Christian lives not out of fear but as a *grateful response* to God's unconditional love. How much holier would our lives be if we lived in gratitude to God rather than in fear of him?

SUGGESTED SCRIPTURE PASSAGES

1 SAMUEL 2:1–10: Hannah's song
PSALM 104: Praise the Lord, O my soul
PSALM 116: What return shall I make for the good
he has done for me?
PSALM 118: You are my God, I will give thanks to you;
I will extol you
PSALM 149:1–5: Praise his name with dancing,
making melody to him
DANIEL 3:52–90: All things bless the Lord
LUKE 1:26–56: Mary's song of gratitude
LUKE 7:36–50: The forgiven woman
LUKE 17:11–19: The grateful leper
1 CORINTHIANS 1:4–9: You are enriched in every way
2 CORINTHIANS 9:6–15: God loves a cheerful giver
PHILIPPIANS 1:3–26: Paul is grateful for his imprisonment
PHILIPPIANS 4:4–13: Rejoice in the Lord, always

GRATEFUL

COLOSSIANS 3:12–17: Give thanks to God
REVELATION 19:5–9: Alleluia! For the Lord our God
the Almighty reigns

PRAYER POINTERS

On a sheet of paper, or perhaps in my journal, I make a graffiti page of random gifts God has given me. I sit prayerfully and simply allow one gift after another to come to mind, and I jot down each one, praising God for the gift.

I zero in on the one gift for which I am most grateful at this moment. It could be the simplest and most trivial of them all. I use that one gift as the springboard of my praise for all that God has done for me.

I reflect on why it is that I do good acts. Is it out of obligation? Fear of God? Or is it grateful response to God's goodness?

I reflect on Psalm 116. I prayerfully consider what would be a grateful response to God for all the good that God has given me. If I feel called to do so, I make a vow to God to respond to his love in some particular and concrete way.

RELATED ENTRIES

Awe, Content, Evening, Joyful, Proud, Can't Wait

WORDS TO TAKE WITH YOU

Life is a banquet, and most of the poor fools
of the world are starving.
—Auntie Mame (paraphrased)

GOD, I'M GRIEVING

The king [David] was deeply moved, and went up to the chamber over the gate, and wept; and as he went, he said, "O my son Absalom, my son, my son Absalom! Would I had died instead of you, O Absalom, my son, my son!"
—2 Samuel 18:33

The experience of grief usually brings about a variety of emotions. It's important to know that when I am grieving, I get to feel anything I want. There is no emotion that I should or should not be feeling. The Lord can make good use of all my emotions, so I do not put any shoulds on my feelings (for example, "I should be feeling sad all the time," or "I should not be angry with God"). I don't even worry if those emotions seem to be contradictory at times. It would be perfectly natural to feel happy and at peace one minute and terribly sad or angry the next. What is important is that, as best I can, I bring this great big jumble of emotions to God. I express to God whatever is in my heart. Since I may find it difficult to focus during this experience, I may find praying through journaling helpful. Putting it on paper may help me to sort through it all.

Part of what we Christians mean when we refer to the communion of saints is that all those saved by God—the canonized saints, my deceased loved ones, and me, too—all of us are part of one living community. This realization might be a great source of consolation to me when I am grieving. My faith tells me that, although not physically present, the one I've loved is right here with me in the room and in my heart. Indeed, since she has reached a state of perfection, she can be present to me in ways more special than when she lived in this world. When I speak to her she will be able to listen to me as never before. And when I reach for her, I know that she embraces me with a love that was not possible before.

Now, that sounds great, but how can I take such words seriously when in reality I feel only emptiness and hear only silence? This might be where the lessons of prayer can help. When I pray, I don't always feel or hear or see anything from God. But in his own way, God makes his presence known to me. In the same way, if I am patient and persistent in prayer, asking for my loved one to come and visit me, I may slowly, subtly begin to sense her presence. It will never be concrete enough to erase the pain of the loss, but it will be enough to get me through another day of grief. It will be enough to keep the sense of withering hopelessness at bay. It will be enough for me to feel loved by her, even now.

SUGGESTED SCRIPTURE PASSAGES

2 SAMUEL 18:33—19:5: Absalom, Absalom, my son, my son

TOBIT 3:1–6: I prayed in anguish

JOB 2:11–13: Job's friends grieve with him

PSALM 90: Lament over human frailty

ECCLESIASTES 3:1–8: There is a time to laugh
and a time to mourn

WISDOM 3:1–9: The souls of the just are in the hand of God

LAMENTATIONS 3: I have seen affliction

MATTHEW 28: Matthew's Resurrection narrative

LUKE 4:16–21: The Spirit of the Lord is upon me
to comfort the mourning

LUKE 6:20–23: Blessed are you who weep now,
for you will laugh

LUKE 22:40–46: Jesus sweats blood in the garden
of Gethsemane

LUKE 23:26–31: Women weep over Jesus' execution

LUKE 24: Luke's Resurrection narrative

JOHN 11:1–44: Jesus grieving over Lazarus

JOHN 20–21: John's Resurrection narrative

1 CORINTHIANS 15:20–28: The last enemy to be destroyed is
death
1 CORINTHIANS 15:50–57: O death, where is your victory?
2 CORINTHIANS 1:3–5: For as our sufferings are abundant, so is
our consolation
1 THESSALONIANS 4:13–18: Those who have fallen asleep

PRAYER POINTERS

I meditate on the Kahlil Gibran quote below. I replay in my imagination all of the delightful moments I've spent with this person.

In prayer I allow myself to feel any emotion that comes. I do
not judge or censor those emotions. I just let them come and
acknowledge their presence before God. I do not try to resolve
my unresolved issues; I just let them be.

I may want to do a lot of journaling at this time. I just write
and write without regard for grammar, spelling or even for
politeness and appropriateness. I just release on paper whatever comes.

If meditating and contemplating are not possible at this
time, I turn to simpler forms of prayer: the rosary, the Liturgy
of the Hours, the Mass, religious music and so on.

If I feel called to do so, I sit quietly and in my heart beg my
beloved to make her presence felt to me. I allow myself to
become very still so that I might notice her presence in the sub-
tlest of ways. If I wish, I might say something to her, or listen to
what she has to say. (Note: this type of prayer may have to come
later in the grieving process. It will probably be too difficult in
the beginning.)

Before I close, I may want to ask God to help me set small
and simple goals for the day, perhaps going a little farther than
yesterday. This may help me to avoid allowing my grief to para-
lyze me.

GRIEVING

RELATED ENTRIES

Angry at You, Change, Dying, Hurt, Sad

WORDS TO TAKE WITH YOU

When you are sorrowful look again in your heart,
and you shall see that in truth you are weeping for
that which has been your delight.
—Kahlil Gibran

GRIEVING

GOD, I FEEL GUILTY

When they had finished breakfast, Jesus said to Simon
Peter, "Simon son of John, do you love me more than
these?" He said to him, "Yes, Lord; you know that I love
you." Jesus said to him, "Feed my lambs." A second time he
said to him, "Simon son of John, do you love me?" He said
to him, "Yes, Lord; you know that I love you." Jesus said to
him, "Tend my sheep." He said to him the third time,
"Simon son of John, do you love me?" Peter felt hurt
because he said to him the third time, "Do you love me?"
And he said to him, "Lord, you know everything; you know
that I love you." Jesus said to him, "Feed my sheep."
—John 21:15–17

Nowadays, we tend to think of feelings of guilt as bad things. We
rightly believe that God wants us to love ourselves and to have
a good self-image; we know that God perceives us as beautiful
and wants us to see ourselves that way, too. But from this prem-
ise, we sometimes wrongly conclude that we should never feel
guilty—that we should dismiss all bad feelings about ourselves
as "Catholic guilt," the last remnants of an outdated worldview.

In moderation guilt can be a healthy thing. In fact, when I
sin, I need guilt to impress upon my psyche that I have hurt
people and have disrupted God's orderly plan of salvation.
Guilt leads me to run back into the merciful arms of God and
to seek reconciliation with those whom I have hurt. It motivates
me to work at never sinning in that way again and prevents me
from judging others. A great deal of the sinfulness of our society today has to do with the fact that we do not consider the
damage we do when we sin. This makes us a selfish people, and
it keeps us from serving God and submitting to his law, God's
blueprint for loving action in the world.

At Jesus' greatest hour of need, Peter, his best friend, denied
three times having known him. Being fully human, Jesus must
have been deeply hurt by this, perhaps more hurt than by the

GUILTY

damage done by the whippers and nailers. And yet, it was not out of revenge but out of love that Jesus forced Peter to face his guilt by having him profess his love for Jesus three times, once for each betrayal. Jesus didn't simply pull him aside and say, "Hey, Peter, I know what you did, but don't worry about it." No, he made Peter experience the pain of remorse. I can't help but wonder what sort of impact this experience of guilt and subsequent forgiveness had on Peter as first pope. Would he have so easily welcomed Paul, who earlier had persecuted Christians? Would he so humbly have laid down his own misgivings about allowing Gentiles to become Christians? Would he so tenderly have cared for his Roman jailers, who faced death because of Peter's escape? Perhaps it was the memory of that painful, guilt-ridden moment on the beach that made the first leader of the church a man of such compassion and mercy, a man who would be remembered by the edict, "Finally, all of you, have unity of spirit, sympathy, love for one another, a tender heart, and a humble mind" (1 Peter 3:8).

SUGGESTED SCRIPTURE PASSAGES

EXODUS 32: The golden calf
2 SAMUEL 12:1–13: David's sin is exposed and he repents
PSALM 32: I said, "I will confess my sins to the Lord,"
and you forgave
PSALM 38: For my sin weighs like a burden too heavy for me
PSALM 51: Wash me, O Lord
PSALM 55:13–15: Betrayed by "my other self"
JEREMIAH 14:17–22: We recognize our wickedness
JONAH 3: Nineveh repents of its sin
MATTHEW 18:6–9: Whoever harms these little ones
LUKE 3:1–14: John the Baptist: "Repent!"
LUKE 7:36–50: The forgiven woman
LUKE 15:11–32: The Prodigal Son

JOHN 4:1–39: The woman at the well
JOHN 8:1–11: The woman being stoned
JOHN 21:15–19: Peter reconciles with Jesus
ACTS 3:11–26: You acted in ignorance
1 JOHN 1:5–10: If we say that we have no sin,
we deceive ourselves

PRAYER POINTERS

In prayer I ask myself, "Is this healthy or unhealthy guilt? Is God working through this guilt to reshape and reform me, or is this guilt from the evil spirit trying to make a bad situation worse?

Assuming my guilt is healthy, I allow myself in prayer to wallow in it for a while. I state before the Lord, in plain English, just how badly I've acted. I explain to the Lord the damage I've done to others. I beg the Lord for forgiveness.

In prayer I ask myself what my life would be like if I could have this fact always before me: I am a sinner, loved and redeemed by God. How would this affect the way I perceive people whom I judge? How would it affect my behavior toward them?

When I feel the calling to do so, I allow the Lord to forgive me, and I ask the Lord to help me to forgive myself.

RELATED ENTRIES

Addicted, Habits, Hate, Sinfully Proud, Sinned

WORDS TO TAKE WITH YOU

Sin is not hurtful because it is forbidden, but it is forbidden because it is hurtful.
—Ben Franklin

You can't really sin until you know that God loves you.
—Dennis Selva

GOD, I'VE GOT BAD HABITS

I do not understand my own actions. For I do not do what
I want, but I do the very thing I hate. Now if I do what I do
not want, I agree that the law is good. But in fact it is no
longer I that do it, but sin that dwells within me. For I
know that nothing good dwells within me, that is, in my
flesh. I can will what is right, but I cannot do it. For I do
not do the good I want, but the evil I do not want is what
I do.... But I see in my members another law at war with
the law of my mind, making me captive to the law of sin
that dwells in my members. Wretched man that I am! Who
will rescue me from this body of death?
—Romans 7:15–19, 23–24

I draw great consolation from the Bible passage above. It helps
me to know that when I am unable to free myself of my bad
habits, at least I'm in good company. That does not excuse me,
of course, from struggling to rid myself of these behaviors, but
it does invite me to experience God's unconditional love for me
just as I am. When I pray about my bad habits, I must allow God
to say to me, "Even if you never transcend this problem, I will
love you anyway." I must pray for the grace to love myself that
much, too. Only standing on the foundation of this unconditional love do I stand a chance of getting better in the habitu-
ally sinful areas of my life.

The second grace to pray for is the grace to see the damage
my behavior does to myself and to those I love. Sin is easy to do
when I make myself ignorant of the hurt that it causes in the
world. When I prayerfully force myself to face the pain I've
caused, I will be less inclined to do it again.

Third, I can ask God to show me ways of protecting those I
hurt in the meantime. I recently put a momma and a daddy
swordtail fish in my aquarium. When the momma became pregnant, the two of them did the most amazing thing. They spent
a couple of days ramming into one of the live plants at the bot-

tom of the tank. They did this so that one by one the branches would break off, float to the surface and form a nest for the baby fish. This nest would provide a hiding place so that the parents wouldn't eat them. Imagine that: the parents built a nest to protect their own offspring from themselves! I must do the same for those I love: I must protect them from myself. Perhaps it will mean that I will have to have a conversation with them, confessing to them my problem and asking them for help with it. When I do hurt others through my bad habits, I will have to go back to them immediately, apologize for it and assure them that the problem is mine, not theirs.

Fourth, I may have to work on my bad habits in bite-sized pieces. In prayer God and I may have to come up with a commitment that I can manage right now, as opposed to one that I know I will not be able to keep. Part of my commitment should be proactive. Instead of merely avoiding sin, I must pursue virtue. For example, if my bad habit is criticizing my spouse throughout the day, then until I lick this problem I could work on giving one compliment for every criticism.

Finally, I must end my prayer as I started, thanking God for loving me just as I am today. Only the assurance of his love can give me the strength I need to work on my bad habits.

SUGGESTED SCRIPTURE PASSAGES

2 KINGS 5:20–27: Gehazi gets greedy
PSALM 51: Wash me, O Lord
MATTHEW 7:1–5: Don't judge others
MATTHEW 7:7–11: Ask and it shall be given you
MATTHEW 7:13–14: Enter by the narrow gate
MARK 9:14–29: This kind can only be cast out through prayer
JOHN 5:1–16: The man at the pool of Bethesda
ROMANS 7:14–25: What I want to do, I do not do
2 CORINTHIANS 12:7–10: My grace is sufficient for you
REVELATION 3:20: Here I am knocking at your door

HABITS

PRAYER POINTERS

In my prayerful imagination, I picture Saint Paul as having the same bad habit as I have. I speak with Paul about it, asking him to show me his heavenly perspective on this situation.

I allow God to tell me that he will love me even if I never resolve this issue in my life.

In humility I reflect on the damage done by my bad habits. I recognize and acknowledge the wounds that I create by these behaviors.

I consider speaking to my loved ones about my bad habits, asking them for forgiveness, advice, companionship and patience.

I commit myself to a small, manageable goal for the day. In prayer I evaluate my performance at the end of each day.

Again, I focus on God's love for me, and I allow that love to inspire me to keep trying. I give thanks for his unconditional love.

RELATED ENTRIES

Addicted, Guilty, Hate, Procrastinator, Sinned

WORDS TO TAKE WITH YOU

God loves me not because I am good
but because God is good.
—Ruth Burrows

GOD, I HATE MYSELF TODAY

> Afterward Job opened his mouth and cursed the day of his
> birth. And Job said, "Let the day perish on which I was to
> be born, and the night which said, 'A boy is conceived.'
> May that day be darkness; Let not God above care for it,
> Nor light shine on it."
> —Job 3:1–4 (NASB)

Noted psychiatrist and Holocaust survivor Viktor Frankl has
dedicated his life to helping depressed people find meaning
and purpose. One of his most intriguing tactics when working
with suicidal people is that he asks the patient, "Why *haven't* you
killed yourself yet?" That sounds like a cruel question, but his
purpose is to show the person that because all these years she
has chosen *not* to kill herself, there must be something inside
her that has a meaning and a purpose—something inside that
knows a reason to live. Our task, Frankl says, is to find that part
of ourselves that has kept us from killing ourselves all along and
to figure out what purpose has fueled that drive for life.

In the same way, if I have chosen to read this particular entry,
then I obviously must *love* myself on some level. Otherwise, why
would I go about the task of finding ways to cure my self-hatred?
My purpose in prayer, then, is to ask the Lord to bring me to
the part of my soul that loved myself enough to get out of bed
this morning, to make myself a cup of coffee, to sit down to
pray, to seek help through this book and this particular entry. I
ask the Lord to bring me to the part of me that deeply loves the
person that I am, just as I am. When I've arrived at that place, I
can then ask myself, "Why have you chosen to live today? What
is it that drives you forward? Why do you love me?"

I suspect that when I find this place in myself, I may well have
found the part of me that is closest to God. It was God, after all,
who loved me first and who placed inside me any love that I possess. And so, perhaps this part of myself that loves me will lead

me to the One who loved me into life, and I can ask my loving Creator those same questions: "If I'm as despicable as I think I am, then why have you, Lord, not chosen to destroy me? Why did you lift my eyelids this morning? Why did you remove last night's headache from me? Why did you have this particular bird sing this particular song by my window? Why, Lord, do you love me?"

And now in prayer, I may need to make a commitment to God. I will commit myself to allow God and that godly, self-loving part of myself to speak kind words to me all day. While driving to work, I promise to allow God to whisper to me, "You are the apple of my eye." When completing a difficult task today, I'll allow that positive part of myself to pat me on the back and say to me, "You're all right, kid." And together God and I will set out on the hard work of forgiving my blunders and shortcomings, and being kind and gentle with the apple of God's eye.

SUGGESTED SCRIPTURE PASSAGES

GENESIS 1—2:4: God's creation: "It is good!"
PSALM 8: What is man that you should care for him?
PSALM 51: Wash me, O Lord
PSALM 139: I praise you that I am wonderfully made
ISAIAH 43:1–8: When you walk through fire,
you shall not be burned
ISAIAH 49:1–18: See, upon the palms of my hands
I've written your name
JEREMIAH 1:4–5: Before I formed you, I knew you
MATTHEW 6:25–34: God cares
MATTHEW 10:26–33: God has counted every hair on your head
LUKE 5:1–11: The call of Simon
LUKE 7:36–50: The forgiven woman

PRAYER POINTERS

In prayer I ask God to take me to the part of myself that loves myself. I go to the part of myself that refuses to give up on me— that loves me that much. In my imagination, I allow that part of myself to explain to me why I am so valuable and lovable.

I reflect on all the tender things the Lord has done for me lately: waking me up this morning, having my friend call me at just the right time, bringing special people into my life and so on. I ask God, "Why do you do these things for me, Lord?" I listen attentively to God's answer.

I commit to God that I will allow God and the self-loving part of myself to speak above the negative voices in my head. I will listen and absorb the loving things that are said to me and about me today.

RELATED ENTRIES

Addicted, Body, Guilty, Habits, Hurt, Jealous, Lust, Single, Sinned

WORDS TO TAKE WITH YOU

The mystery of human existence lies not in just staying alive, but in finding something to live for.
—Dostoevsky

GOD, I'VE BEEN HURT
BY OTHERS

Surely he has borne our infirmities
and carried our diseases;
yet we accounted him stricken,
struck down by God, and afflicted.
But he was wounded for our transgressions,
crushed for our iniquities;
upon him was the punishment that made us whole,
and by his bruises we are healed.
—Isaiah 53:4–5

Before I became a priest I always imagined that the most moving part of the Mass as a presider would be the moment of consecration when I lift high the Body and Blood of Jesus. But now that I am a priest, it is another moment of lifting that moves me more: the lifting of the broken Body of Christ after the fraction rite of the Mass. After living my whole life as a Catholic and a Christian, this fundamental pillar of our faith never ceases to confound and mystify me. What a strange religion that worships a broken God! No other religion is so audacious as to believe in a God who loves his puny little creations so much that he would choose to rescue them from their own deserved wretchedness by becoming one of them and by joining them precisely in their wretchedness and brokenness. I can hardly believe it myself. And yet, again and again, I find myself at God's altar, lifting that broken Body and proclaiming, "This is the Lamb of God."

When I have been wounded, I have three people to whom I may turn: I could turn to the one who hurt me, I could turn to myself, or I could turn to *the* Wounded One: Christ crucified, and yet resurrected. I go to Mass in order to choose Christ. I go to profess the belief and hope that God could have really done it: that God could have graced woundedness with his own presence, thereby making it a sacred instrument of my salvation. I go to Mass because I want to do with my wounded self what Jesus did with his: "Into your hands, Lord, I commend my spirit." I, too, must commend my wounded spirit so that the Father will raise me also. Just as the Father glorified the broken body of Jesus, so will the Father do with my brokenness, if I only surrender myself to him.

Only *after* I have given over my woundedness to the Father can I turn to my perpetrators. If I do so before, I may well find myself either seeking revenge or putting myself in harm's way again, neither of which would be Christ's way. And only after I have given over my woundedness to the Father, can I begin the slow process of healing. If I do so before, I may well become forever lost in my woundedness, never to look beyond myself again. I may well seek relief in gods that will only leave me more wounded, in substance abuse, self-pity, revenge, self-hatred or denial.

> Come to me all you that are weary and are carrying heavy burdens, and I will give you rest.
> (Matthew 11:28–30)

SUGGESTED SCRIPTURE PASSAGES

GENESIS 37:1–36; 42:1—45:28: The story of Joseph
2 SAMUEL 16:5–14: Absalom seeking David's death
PSALM 55:13–15: Betrayed by "my other self"
ISAIAH 53:3–5: It was our sufferings that he endured
MATTHEW 5:38–48: Do not retaliate; love your enemies.
MATTHEW 10:26–39: Brother will fight with brother
MATTHEW 18:21–35: Forgive seventy-seven times
LUKE 22–23: Luke's Passion narrative
LUKE 23:33–49: Forgive them, Father….
ACTS 5:40–42: The disciples for their part left rejoicing
ACTS 7:54–60: Stephen's martyrdom
✓ROMANS 12:9–21: Be at peace with all; vengeance is mine

HURT

✓1 CORINTHIANS 1:18–25: I preach Christ crucified
✓ CORINTHIANS 4:9–13: We are fools on Christ's account
✓2 TIMOTHY 4:9–18: Everyone has abandoned me

PRAYER POINTERS

I reflect on the broken body of Jesus. I meditate on Jesus' twisted and bleeding body as he hung on the cross. I let him speak to me from the cross. I listen carefully to what he has to say.

I reflect on Jesus' gift of his own body and blood. I sit with Jesus and the apostles on the night of the Last Supper and I watch and listen as Jesus turns to me offering me the cup and saying, "Take this. This is my blood which will be shed for you." I reflect how I am not alone in my suffering; Jesus accompanies me as I go through this difficult period. I may want to do such a reflection while praying before the blessed sacrament.

I set my three options before me: I see that I could turn toward my perpetrators, toward myself or toward Christ. Using my imagination, I imagine how my life would go if I focus my energies and attentions on my perpetrators. What kind of person would I become? Now, I imagine how my life would go if I turn toward myself. What kind of person would I become? Now, I imagine how my life would go if I turn toward the suffering, crucified and resurrected Christ. What kind of person would I become?

RELATED ENTRIES

Angry, Confront, Forgive, Jealous, Judgmental, Sad

WORDS TO TAKE WITH YOU

Jesus did not come to explain away suffering or remove it. He came to fill it with his presence.
—Paul Claudel

GOD, I'M JEALOUS

> Now Israel loved Joseph more than any other of his chil-
> dren, because he was the son of his old age; and he had
> made him a long robe with sleeves. But when his brothers
> saw that their father loved him more than all his brothers,
> they hated him, and could not speak peaceably to him....
> So when Joseph came to his brothers, they stripped him of
> his robe, the long robe with sleeves that he wore; and they
> took him and threw him into a pit.
> —Genesis 37:3–4, 23–24

After five years of study and spiritual formation in the Society of
Jesus, I received my first long-term, full-time job. I was to be a
high school teacher and counselor at Jesuit College
Preparatory in Dallas. Needless to say, it was extremely important to me that I perform well. A great deal was riding on my
success or failure. I had never taught before in my life and
could not have been more nervous. I remember that on my first
day, I had forgotten to wear a belt and watched with horror as
various students throughout the day received PHs (Penance
Hall slips) for not wearing theirs!

One of my best friends in the Jesuits, Dino, was assigned to
Jesuit Prep that same year. Dino and I had entered the Jesuits on
the exact same day and had lived in the same communities for
four of our five years in the Society. He is an extraordinarily fun
and friendly guy and the kids at Jesuit Prep took to him like bees
to honey. During many lunchtimes and free periods, Dino
would have a swarm of students in his office, laughing and car-
rying on with him. My office was next door and sometimes, as I
tried to grade papers or plan lessons, I could hear the good-spir-
ited fun through the paper-thin wall that separated our offices.

Now, looking back on that period several years ago, I can
objectively say that I had my fair share of students who liked to
hang out with me. More importantly, now, in my seventh year of

high school teaching and my sixteenth year in the Jesuits, my popularity rating among adolescents is not the greatest factor in how I evaluate the success of my work. But back then, any day that Dino had adoring fans in his office and I didn't was a day of failure in my mind. I can't fully describe the blow I felt as I uselessly tried to focus on my work on those days. Following on the heels of this rush of jealousy was the guilt of having such selfish and petty thoughts. I wanted so badly to be happy for my friend, to praise God for his giftedness and to thank God for calling him to minister as a Jesuit. I wanted to go inside that office and join in the fun. But instead, I sat with my papers and red pen, sulking and licking the wounds of my foolish pride.

My salvation came not in solving the problem and becoming completely free of jealousy, but rather in my acknowledgment of this problem in prayer. After doing so, it became a sort of joke for God and me. I used those feelings of jealousy to remind me of what a little boy I still was and how much I needed my father-God to tell that me I'm all right, just as I am. Then with my will, if not with my heart, I could praise God for the giftedness of my friend and pray that all of his gifts would grow ever stronger and ever more effective in ministering to God's people.

SUGGESTED SCRIPTURE PASSAGES

GENESIS 27:1–45, 33:1–20: Jacob and Esau

GENESIS 37:1–36, 42:1—45:28: The story of Joseph

MATTHEW 18:1–5: Who is the greatest?

MATTHEW 20:1–16: Are you jealous because I am generous?

MATTHEW 20:20–28: Let us sit at your right

LUKE 15:11–32: Prodigal son's brother

JOHN 21:20–23: Peter is jealous of the beloved disciple

1 CORINTHIANS 1:10—2:5: Paul addresses factions:
I came in weakness

1 CORINTHIANS 3: For as long as there is jealousy,
are you not of the flesh?

1 CORINTHIANS 12:4–31: All have different gifts
1 CORINTHIANS 12:31—13:13: Love is not jealous
JAMES 4:1–12: Jealousy leads to war

PRAYER POINTERS

I acknowledge to God in prayer my jealous feelings. I "come clean" about how childishly I envy the other person's gifts. If I receive the grace to do so, I laugh with Jesus about my silly childishness.

With my will, if not with my heart, I earnestly praise God for the giftedness of the person of whom I'm envious. I describe to God in detail just how impressive this person's strengths are, and I praise God for God's fine craftsmanship in creating this particular person.

Sometimes it's good to have a conversation with the person and let him or her know about my jealousy. It might help just to get everything out in the open. In prayer I can ask God whether or not this would be a good idea.

I allow God to show me my own giftedness, however meek it may appear to me at this moment. I trust that in God's eyes, I am just as special; I am the apple of his eye.

RELATED ENTRIES

Body, Hate, Hurt, Judgmental, Sinned

WORDS TO TAKE WITH YOU

What would be the cost of not having an enemy?
—Charles Frazier, *Cold Mountain*

Blessed are they who laugh at themselves. They shall never cease to be entertained.
—Chinese Proverb

GOD, I'M JOYFUL

And Mary said,
"My soul magnifies the Lord,
    and my spirit rejoices in God my Savior,
for he has looked with favor on the lowliness of his servant.
    Surely, from now on all generations will call me blessed;
for the Mighty One has done great things for me,
    and holy is his name."
—Luke 1:46–49

In her novel, *Dinner at Homesick Restaurant*, Anne Tyler tells a story about an unhappy woman named Pearl Tull. Now blind and near the end of her life, she asks her son Ezra to read aloud the entries from her childhood diaries. He assumed she simply enjoyed reminiscing about her past. But one day...

> He riffled through the pages, glimpsing buttonhole stitch and watermelon social and set of fine furs for $22.50. "Early this morning," he read to his mother, "I went out behind the house to weed. Was kneeling in the dirt by the stable with my pinafore a mess and the perspiration rolling down my back, wiped my face on my sleeve, reached for the trowel, and all at once thought, Why I believe that at just this moment I am absolutely happy."
>
> His mother stopped rocking and grew very still.
>
> "The Bedloe girl's piano scales were floating out her window," he read, "and a bottle fly was buzzing in the grass, and I saw that I was kneeling on such a beautiful green little planet. I don't care what else might come about, I have had this moment. It belongs to me."
>
> That was the end of the entry. He fell silent.
>
> "Thank you, Ezra," his mother said. "There's no need to read any more."

As a spiritual director I have the privilege of hearing about ecstatic times in people's lives—moments of falling in love, of finding one's true vocation in life, of extraordinary prayer experiences, of tremendous successes and of feeling loved and accepted. But staying with these people as the months and years go on, I also hear about darker times. In those times people sometimes mistakenly perceive their entire lives as dark and unhappy. When I remind them of joyful moments they've shared with me, they often dismiss them as delusional and unreal.

Saint Ignatius Loyola advised that when in consolation I should prepare for desolation. He was not being morbid and was not advising that I spoil a joyful moment by reminding myself that there are more troubles to come. Instead, he said this because he knew from experience that doubt and cynicism might set in all too soon. How, then, do I use this joy to prepare for desolation? The most important way is to be as faithful to prayer during the joyful times of my life as I am when I am in trouble. This may be difficult to do; I tend to turn to God more often during times of distress than during happy times. But to prepare for desolation, I should take my joy to prayer. I should praise God for it and ask God to show me ways that I might use this joy to bring about true growth and lasting peace in my life.

SUGGESTED SCRIPTURE PASSAGES

PSALM 23: The Lord is my shepherd
PSALM 126: They shall return rejoicing
PSALM 149:1–5: Praise him with dancing,
making melody with tambourine
ISAIAH 55:1–13: All who are thirsty, come to the water
LUKE 1:26–56: Mary's song of joy; John the Baptist
leaping in the womb
LUKE 10:17–24: Rejoice that your names
are recorded in heaven

JOHN 15:9–17: That your joy may be complete
PHILIPPIANS 4:4–13: Rejoice in the Lord always
REVELATION 4:1–11: Angels praising God
REVELATION 21:1–5: Behold, I make all things new

PRAYER POINTERS

In prayer I do as Pearl Tull did: I write a journal entry all about the joy that I feel, describing every detail of it. This entry will be undeniable evidence for the darker moments in my life when I am tempted to dismiss my joyful times as delusional.

I spend a great deal of time praising God for this moment and every little detail of it. If I were Pearl, I would praise God for the soil, the piano scales, the trowel and so on.

I imagine either the face of God the Father or the face of Jesus. I picture the broad smile on his face and see how delighted he is to see me so happy.

RELATED ENTRIES

Awe, Content, Evening, Grateful, Proud, Can't Wait

WORDS TO TAKE WITH YOU

God is a comedian, playing for an audience
too afraid to laugh.
—Francois Voltaire

The Lord is good, when we adjust
ourselves to his supreme sense of humor!
—Theresa Richard

GOD, I'VE BEEN JUDGMENTAL LATELY

> Do not judge, so that you may not be judged. For with the
> judgment you make you will be judged, and the measure
> you give will be the measure you get.
> —Matthew 7:1–2

Wanna hear a joke? OK, so the priest takes a seat in a crowded subway car. An inebriated-looking homeless man stumbles in and sits in the only seat left, the one beside the priest. The perturbed priest begins to think judgmental thoughts about his seatmate and huffily opens his newspaper to avoid speaking to him. After a minute or two, the homeless man asks the priest, "Say, do you know what causes arthritis?" The priest testily snaps back, "Drunkenness, laziness and licentiousness." The homeless man said, "Is that right?" with great surprise and concern. Another minute or two passes, and the priest begins to feel guilty for what he's done. "I'm sorry, Mister," he says in a soothing voice, "Tell me about your struggle with arthritis." "Oh I don't have arthritis," says the man, and then pointing to the priest's newspaper he said, "I was just noticing this headline that said the pope has arthritis."

Looking through the Gospels, it is easy to see that practically the only thing Jesus ever really got hopping mad about was the judgmental attitude of the religious folk of the day. With criminals, sexual deviants, tax collectors and Samaritans, Jesus was gentle and patient, but he couldn't stand to see religious people heaping damnations on others. That should tell me something about how serious it is to judge another and how important it is that I work on ridding myself of this behavior. Sometimes judgmental thoughts well up inside me, despite my best intentions. That, in and of itself, is not a sin. Nor is it necessarily a sin to acknowledge the wrongdoing of another or even to seek retribution. But I do sin when I think or talk badly of someone with the intention of putting that person down—of smearing the person's character. If I find myself doing this often, I'll need to take it to prayer.

As a Jesuit I spent almost a year once going back and forth between ministering to prisoners in the "murder unit" of a large county jail and ministering to parishioners at a beautiful blue-collar Catholic parish. One day, while working with a deeply remorseful young man in the prison, it struck me that there was only one essential difference between these two populations: *the prisoners knew who they were.* Their sins were public knowledge and every moment of their lives they were reminded of it. Therefore, they approached God with great humility and great joy at the thought that God forgives and loves unconditionally. Meanwhile, the parishioners (and I, too) could often create the unconscious illusion that we had no problems and that we had somehow earned God's love. It's ironic, isn't it? This essential difference led to an experience of *liberation* in the prisoners' lives that many of us "free people" never have. And nothing reminds me of the prison of my own sinfulness more than when I acknowledge my sin of a judgmental heart.

Have mercy, Lord, even on the unmerciful.

SUGGESTED SCRIPTURE PASSAGES

PSALM 51: Wash me, O Lord
MATTHEW 7:1–5: Don't judge others
MARK 2:13–17: I have come for the sinners, not the righteous
MARK 15:22–32: He saved others.
Why doesn't he save himself?
LUKE 15:11–32: Prodigal son's brother
LUKE 18:9–14: The publican and the Pharisee
LUKE 18:15–17: Let the children come to me
LUKE 21:1–4: The widow's mite

JOHN 8:1–11: The woman being stoned
ROMANS 2:1–4: The standard by which you judge
COLOSSIANS 3:12–17: Bear with one another
HEBREWS 5:2: Because he himself was beset by weakness
JAMES 4:7–12: Do not judge your neighbor

PRAYER POINTERS

First, I ask God to help me see the situation from a more objective point of view. Maybe there are good reasons for the person's behavior. Saint Ignatius Loyola implores his followers to put the best possible spin on any situation—to assume the best in people.

If it's clear that a person has done something sinful—and that's a big *if*—it should break my heart, not make me smug. I should, of course, pray for anyone who has been hurt by this person's actions, but I should also ask God to show me the hurt that this person has caused *himself* and pray for his well being. Perceiving the sinner as wounded does not excuse him from his actions, but it helps me to understand his actions and to love him precisely because he is in great need of love—it is to these that Jesus came (Mark 2:13–17).

Finally, I pray for forgiveness for my judgmental heart. I allow the Lord to show me how damaging my own attitudes are and beg the Lord to reform and reshape my heart into an unconditionally loving one.

RELATED ENTRIES

Blew Up, Confront, Forgive, Jealous, Sinfully Proud, Sinned

WORDS TO TAKE WITH YOU

We are never so serious as when we joke.
—Anonymous

Every devil I meet is an angel in disguise.
—The Indigo Girls

For some, the Church doesn't have them, but God does. For some, the Church has them, but God doesn't.
—Saint Augustine

No one knows whose womb bears the chief.
—Ancient African Proverb

Indeed in nothing is the power of the Dark Lord more clearly shown than in the estrangement that divides all those who still oppose him.
—J. R. R. Tolkien, *The Fellowship of the Ring*

JUDGMENTAL

GOD, I'M LONELY

How lovely is your dwelling place,
O LORD of hosts!
My soul longs, indeed it faints
for the courts of the LORD;
my heart and my flesh sing for joy
to the living God.
Even the sparrow finds a home,
and the swallow a nest for herself,
where she may lay her young,
at your altars, O LORD of hosts,
my King and my God.
Happy are those who live in your house,
ever singing your praise.
...
For a day in your courts is better
than a thousand elsewhere.
I would rather be a doorkeeper in the house of my God
than live in the tents of wickedness.
—Psalm 84:1–4, 10

OK, ready for a Cajun vocabulary lesson? Cajuns are Louisiana French-Canadians who have their own words and expressions mixed in with English. For example, as I child, I was told not to *boude* (pronounced *bu dey*), because Santa Claus is coming soon. While other American barefooted boys might step on a thorn, I would be careful not to step on a *peekon* (pronounced *pee kanh*). And if I was a mischievous lad, my grandmother might exclaim, with a slight smile, "He's so *canaille* (pronounced *kah nahy*)!"

Sometimes my mother would be struck with a sudden *envie* (pronounced *anh vee*). That is, she had a terrible craving for some particular food or drink. I remember as teenagers my brother and I would have to drive all around our little town late in the evening searching for a pop machine that sold Mr. Pibb, the frequent object of my mother's *envies* ("No, Dr. Pepper just won't do!"). It was a great opportunity to return a little of the lavish love Mom had for us, but, of course, that didn't stop us from teasing her about her wild cravings. We blamed it on her seven pregnancies!

One Cajun word that seems to have no English equivalent is *tracas* (pronounced *trah kah*). To have a *tracas* is to have an unidentifiable *envie*. We had a cat once who often had a *tracas*. He would go to his food dish and eat a bite or two, but without real enthusiasm. He would lie down for a nap, but then get up again very soon. He would paw the door indicating that he wanted to go outside, but when we opened the door, he would sit right against the door frame, keeping his options open by preventing us from closing the door again. A person with a *tracas* might amble around the house opening and closing the fridge, picking up and putting down the phone receiver, restlessly surfing television channels.

I experience loneliness as a spiritual *tracas*. I have a strong *envie* for something, but can't figure out what might be the object of my desire. Nothing seems to quench this unidentifiable thirst. But perhaps Saint Augustine's oft-quoted words, "Our hearts are restless, Lord, until they rest in you" are so often quoted because they identify for all of us the object of our spiritual *tracas*. Perhaps at its heart, loneliness is my soul's longing to return to God, its source and origin. My *envie*, my deep thirst, is for God himself. Sometimes then, during periods of loneliness, I might choose not to remedy my loneliness with TV, work or even with friends. Instead, I turn to prayer; I delve deep into that longing of my soul, and beg God to fill that empty space with his presence. Nothing else will do.

SUGGESTED SCRIPTURE PASSAGES

EXODUS 33:7–17: The Lord to Moses:
"You are my intimate friend"
1 KINGS 19: Elijah visited by the Lord: "I alone am left"

RUTH 1:1–18: Ruth is loyal to her mother-in-law
PSALM 22: I am a worm, despised by the people
PSALM 84: Even the sparrow finds a home
PSALM 88: My only companion is darkness
DANIEL 6:1–23: Daniel in the lions' den
MATTHEW 8:18–22: The Son of Man has nowhere
to lay his head
MATTHEW 28:16–20: I am with you to the end
LUKE 4:1–13: Jesus in the desert
LUKE 15:11–32: The Prodigal Son
LUKE 22–23: Luke's Passion narrative
LUKE 22:40–46: Jesus sweats blood in the garden of
Gethsemane.
2 CORINTHIANS 12:7–10: My grace is sufficient for you
2 TIMOTHY 4:9–18: Everyone has abandoned me

PRAYER POINTERS

Instead of running from my loneliness, I cherish this moment as an opportunity to spend intimate time with my Lord. I turn off my phone, TV and computer. I make a pot of coffee or tea. I put on my favorite sweatshirt.

In prayer I allow myself to feel Jesus' presence in the room. I ask him to come closer and notice how readily he does so. We sit together, hand in hand or arms around each other's shoulders, whatever feels comfortable.

Saint Augustine says, "Our hearts are restless, Lord, until they rest in you." I ask Jesus to fill this empty place in my heart, and I reflect on how only he can truly bring me peace and rest.

RELATED ENTRIES

Dry, Hurt, Lost, Quiet, Sad, Single

WORDS TO TAKE WITH YOU

All man's miseries derive from his inability
to sit alone in a room.
—Blaise Pascal

Life is full of those damp little moments of gloom
that come and go. They mean nothing.
—Anne Tyler, *Morgan's Passing*

LONELY

GOD, I FEEL LOST

Some wandered in desert wastes,
  finding no way to an inhabited town;
hungry and thirsty,
  their soul fainted within them.
Then they cried to the LORD in their trouble,
  and he delivered them from their distress;
he led them by a straight way,
  until they reached an inhabited town.
Let them thank the LORD for his steadfast love,
  for his wonderful works to humankind.
—Psalm 107:4–8

As uncomfortable as it may be, being lost is often a healthy stage in any process. When I began to write this book, I spent a great deal of time seemingly completely lost. It took an interminable amount of time—from my perspective anyway—to stumble through various samples of bad writing before I found the right rhythm. But all writers know that this is a healthy and perhaps necessary stage in the writing process. One must grope and fumble and then retreat and come back to try again and again and again. One writer, Lawrence Kushner, says that just as the singer must clear her throat before singing, so must the writer hack and cough up bad material before he begins to "sing." This alone would be a difficult experience if there were smooth sailing from that point forward, but in reality there are lots of new beginnings within the process, and each one begins with this awkward and uncomfortable feeling of not knowing what the heck I'm doing.

Practically every worthy endeavor contains these phases of lostness. It is simply a part of the human condition to spend some difficult time unsure of where one is and of where one is headed. Should this be the case in my present situation, then in my prayer I shouldn't begin with the presumption that being lost is a bad thing and that the Lord does not will for me to be here. There is a great deal that the Lord can teach me in this state. The desert can be a time of formation. God required the Israelites to wander through the desert for forty years. Why? Maybe because there simply were lessons that they had to learn in the wasteland before they would be ready to enter the Promised Land. Like the Israelites, I'm tempted to lose heart in those times—to abandon the dream and return to the enslavement of yesterday. In my prayer then, I must fortify myself. I must say my creed, professing my faith that God has much work to do within me as I wander, seemingly aimlessly.

On the other hand, the Lord may be waiting for me to ask him to take the wheel! To be lost is to recognize the fact that I'm not in control—that a Higher Power must drive the car if we'll ever get there. In my prayer I may discover that the only reason I'm lost is that I've refused to give God the car keys. If I feel it is my own state of sinfulness or stubbornness that has got me lost, then this might be a good time for me to deepen my surrendering to Jesus, the Lord and Savior of my life. This, too, is a process that must be repeated again and again throughout my Christian journey.

SUGGESTED SCRIPTURE PASSAGES

1 KINGS 3:1–15: Solomon asks for wisdom
PSALM 23: The Lord is my shepherd
PSALM 107:4–9: The people are led into the Promised Land
PSALM 130: Out of the depths I cry to you, O Lord
PSALM 139:1–18: If I wander to the sea, you are there
WISDOM 9:1–11: Give me wisdom that sits by your throne
ISAIAH 42:1–16: I will lead the blind by paths unknown
MATTHEW 9:35–38: They were like sheep without a shepherd
MATTHEW 18:10–14: Leaving the ninety-nine sheep
to seek the lost one

MARK 4:35–41: Jesus sleeps while the sea storm rages
LUKE 2:41–52: Finding the child Jesus in the Temple
LUKE 15: Lost sheep; lost coin; lost son
JOHN 10:1–18: I am the Good Shepherd
JOHN 14:1–14: Lord, we do not know the way
ACTS 27:6–44: Paul lost at sea

PRAYER POINTERS

In my prayer I imagine myself lost in a forest, a desert or some other appropriate metaphor for my current situation. I call out to Christ, using the mantra, "Find me, Lord" or "Lead me home, Lord."

I ask the Lord to reveal to me what things I might learn while in this state of being lost. How might the Lord use this as an opportunity to save me, teach me, heal me, nurture me and so on?

Often I am lost because I'm too stubborn to ask for help from others. I should pray over the questions, "Am I lost because I'm trying too hard to go it alone? Who might be helpful to me right now? What's keeping me from asking for help?"

Often we feel lost when we cannot articulate what exactly is our destination. I should spend some time with my prayer journal, asking God to help me compose a series of mission statements that become increasingly more concrete and particular. For example, I might start with, "My mission is to live my life according to God's will." I might spend a whole prayer time on that one statement. Then, the next day, I might write, "My mission is to be a good mother to my children." Then, later, "My mission is to help my seventeen-year-old to adopt a mature attitude about alcohol." And still later, "My mission right now is to talk to my son, heart-to-heart." I should proceed in this way until I have to a concrete plan with which to act.

My Lord God, I have no idea where I am going. I do not see

the road ahead of me. I cannot know for certain where it will end. Nor do I really know myself, and the fact that I think that I am following your will does not mean that I am actually doing so. But I believe that the desire to please you does in fact please you. And I hope I have that desire in all that I am doing. I hope that I will never do anything apart from that desire. And I know that if I do this, you will lead me by the right road though I may know nothing about it. Therefore will I trust you always though I may seem to be lost and in the shadow of death. I will not fear, for you are ever with me, and you will never leave me to face my perils alone.
—"A Prayer for the Lost Journeyman," Thomas Merton

RELATED ENTRIES

Change, Decide, Despair, Doubts, Dry, Lonely, Nighttime, Sad

WORDS TO TAKE WITH YOU

Not all those who wander are lost.
—J. R. R. Tolkien

Lost is a place, too.
—Christina Crawford

GOD, I'M IN LOVE

The voice of my beloved!
Look, he comes,
leaping upon the mountains,
bounding over the hills.
My beloved is like a gazelle
or a young stag.
Look, there he stands
behind our wall,
gazing in at the windows,
looking through the lattice.
My beloved speaks and says to me:
"Arise, my love, my fair one,
and come away."
—Song of Solomon 2:8–10

I was recently at the home of friends who have been married for quite some time. At one point the three of us were standing around the kitchen chatting when the wife put lotion on her hands and started rubbing them. A moment later she walked over to her husband with her outstretched arms and said, "Here, Jim, I've put too much lotion. Take some." Jim obediently stuck out his hands and the four hands met and kissed and caressed each other. I was so struck by the simple beauty of the moment that it took my breath away, and I forgot whatever it was I was saying. And for that long moment while their hands were joined, I was no longer in the room. It was only these two lovers and their hands comfortably kneading each other. The moment passed and the two of them looked up at me as I stared stupidly at the spot in the room where their hands had just met. I finally looked at the wife and said, "My mom used to do the exact same thing." She smiled a knowing smile and said, "I'm always putting too much lotion on my hands; it gives me an excuse to touch him." And then the husband put a grimace on his face as he smelled his hands and said, "Now, I smell like—"

"Like a girrrrrl," his wife finished for him, and they both laughed like the childish lovers that they were.

When one is in love, it is as though God has maxed-out the dial labeled "Wonder and Awe" on his creation machine. All colors are richer, all noises become music, all people seem to exist to keep the loved one occupied until the beloved comes back into the room. Falling in love is the easy and fun part. The tricky and labor-intensive part is to turn that original dream world into a long-term love that will still be around when God's Wonder and Awe dial is turned back down to normal. This will require a great deal of prayerful discernment.

When I have fallen in love, the temptation both in prayer and in life would be simply to allow this dreamy vessel of love to take me wherever it wills. But that would not be God's will. When I fall in love, I lose my sense of judgment and objectivity and therefore I'm in a vulnerable state in which I may make tragic mistakes that I can't reverse. Besides praising God for this indescribable gift, I will need to roll up my spiritual sleeves and get to work in my prayer life. I have some tough questions on which to reflect. Where am I going in this relationship? Is this really the person I'm meant to spend my life with? What values do I need to protect and preserve as I journey down this road? What person or persons are wise and trustworthy enough to help me discern things as the love progresses?

Falling in love is a beautiful gift, but as with many gifts, there is some assembly required.

SUGGESTED SCRIPTURE PASSAGES

GENESIS 2:18–24: This at last is bone of my bone,
flesh of my flesh
GENESIS 29:9–11: Jacob and Rachel
SONG OF SOLOMON: The entire book is a love poem
MATTHEW 5:1–12: Blessed are the pure in spirit

MATTHEW 7:24–27: Build your house on rock
MATTHEW 22:35–40: Greatest commandment: love God with
your whole heart
JOHN 15:9–12: That your joy may be complete,
remain in my love
ROMANS 12:1–2: Offer your bodies as a sacrifice; do not conform to this age
ROMANS 12:9–12: Let your love be sincere
1 CORINTHIANS 12:31—13:13: Love is…
1 JOHN 3:18–24: Our love is not to be mere talk

PRAYER POINTERS

I spend a lot of time in prayer thanking and praising God for this wonderful experience of love.

I ask God to help me set down on paper the values I wish to protect and preserve as I take this journey. What are the decisions I've made in my life that cannot be compromised?

With Jesus at my side, I allow myself to fantasize about my future with this person. I ask Jesus to show me the problematic aspects of a future with this person, and I discuss these potential problems with Jesus.

I ask God to help me find two or three wise and loving people who could guide me through this journey. I commit to God that I will be completely honest with these people and that I will listen to what they have to say about it.

After speaking with these wise and loving people, I take their responses to prayer. I ask God to help me learn and grow from what they've had to say.

RELATED ENTRIES

Awe, Content, Grateful, Joyful, Lust, Sexually Aroused,
Can't Wait

WORDS TO TAKE WITH YOU

Love is a splendidly useless passion.
—Thomas Green, *Opening to God*

The one who fears love fears life.
—Ballykissangel

Lost is a place, too.
—Christina Crawford

LOVE

GOD, I'M IN LUST

Therefore God gave them up in the lusts of their hearts to impurity, to the degrading of their bodies among themselves, because they exchanged the truth about God for a lie and worshiped and served the creature rather than the Creator, who is blessed forever! Amen.
—Romans 1:24–25

A teenager confesses to the priest that he's had lustful thoughts. The priest asks, "Have you been *entertaining* those thoughts?" "No, Father," the boy responds, "They've been entertaining me!" This little joke alludes to the distinction between lust and sexual arousal. Sexual arousal is a biological response when stimulated by an arousing stimulus. In and of itself, it is not a sin. In fact, it is a part of God's gift of sexuality. Lust is when I take those sexual thoughts and feelings and *choose to dwell* on them—when I *entertain* those thoughts. I let them consume me, all the while reducing the person I'm lusting after into an object to be used for my own physical pleasure. It is important to understand this distinction because many good people feel guilty about merely being sexually aroused. Even if they choose not to dwell on or act upon their sexual feelings, they still feel as though they've done something wrong. In the process they have set impossible standards for themselves, and living a good Christian life becomes an unrealistic endeavor.

So the first question I must ask myself in prayer is, "Am I lusting or am I merely sexually aroused?" If it is the latter, I should go to that section of the book: "God, I'm Sexually Aroused." If it is the former, I should read on.

In *The Theology of the Body* Pope John Paul II has said that the problem with pornography is *not* that it shows too much but that it shows too little. The problem is that they show only a tiny part of all that is wonderful about the person in the picture, and even that one aspect is distorted because it is out of the

LUST

context of the beauty of the whole person. Lust, then, is a sin not because we look too much at another person, but because we don't look well enough. In prayer I might hear God saying to me, "If you think her body is nice, wait until you see what *I* see in her!" To pray about lust, then, is to ask the Lord to restore the whole picture of the person.

If lust is a chronic problem for me, then I need prayerfully to get at the root of it. Whereas healthy spousal sex is a mutual sharing that longs for the happiness and pleasure of the other as much as one's own, lustful thoughts and feelings are often about power and domination. The root problem, then, seems to be that of a poor self-image, since anyone with a healthy self-image has no need to play power games. Because chronic lust is ultimately a symptom of low self-esteem, I first need to ask God to help me to perceive myself as God sees me. Doing so will both uplift and humble me. Only then will I be able to begin to see others through God's eyes.

SUGGESTED SCRIPTURE PASSAGES

JUDGES 16:4–31: Samson's lust destroys him
2 SAMUEL 11: David and Bathsheba
MATTHEW 14:3–12: Herod and Salome
ROMANS 1:18–32: On lust
ROMANS 12:1–2: Offer your bodies as a sacrifice;
do not conform to this age
1 CORINTHIANS 6:9–20: Your body is a temple of the Holy Spirit
1 CORINTHIANS 10:12–14: God will not test you
beyond your strength
GALATIANS 5:13–25: You are called for freedom
EPHESIANS 4:17–24: Put on a new self
COLOSSIANS 3:1–10: Think of the higher things
1 THESSALONIANS 4:1–8: Control your own body
in holiness and honor
1 JOHN 2:12–17: Do not love the enticements of the world

PRAYER POINTERS

I prayerfully discern my actions. Using the distinction above, I ask myself, am I really lusting or merely sexually aroused?

If this is a serious and chronic problem, I pray about what I can do to change the circumstances of my life that lead to lust. Do I look at movies, TV shows, books, magazines or Web sites that lead me into lustful thoughts and actions? If so, I do whatever is necessary to get rid of those temptations.

I pray about the beauty of God's creation. If there is a particular person I am lusting after, I ask God to show me what he sees in this person—to show me the beauty of the whole person, not just this person's physical features.

I ask God to help me to "think of the higher things," as Saint Paul puts it. I reflect on what those "higher things" might be in my life and what "high things" God might be calling me to right now in my life.

I ask God to show me how he sees me—to show me just how beautiful I am in God's eyes. I reflect on the fact that my whole self is a temple of the Holy Spirit.

RELATED ENTRIES

Addicted, Awe, Habits, Hate, Lonely, Love, Sexually Aroused, Sinned

WORDS TO TAKE WITH YOU

The human mind is a continuously working factory of idols.
—John Calvin

We ought, so far as in us lies, to put on Immortality, and do all that we can to live in conformity with the Highest that is in us.
—Aristotle

GOD, THIS MARRIAGE STUFF IS TOUGH

> As God's chosen ones, holy and beloved, clothe yourselves with compassion, kindness, humility, meekness, and patience. Bear with one another and, if anyone has a complaint against another, forgive each other; just as the Lord has forgiven you, so you also must forgive. Above all, clothe yourselves with love, which binds everything together in perfect harmony. And let the peace of Christ rule in your hearts, to which indeed you were called in the one body.
> —Colossians 3:12–15

If I reach the point where I am at the end of my rope with my spouse, there are many different ways to take it to prayer.

I could ask the Lord to show me just how much my spouse means to me. I reflect back on all the great things he has done for me over the years, and I thank God for each gift.

I could ask the Lord to show me ways to communicate my love for him. For the sake of keeping the marriage fresh, I may perhaps need to come up with new ways of doing so. Maybe I could do so through a letter, or through a small gift. I could perhaps think of a kind but simple gesture such as working a little harder on the family chores. I could seek more opportunities to give simple and quiet compliments.

I could pray for my spouse, lifting him up in my prayers and asking the Lord's blessing on him.

I could ask the Lord to show me ways that *I* irritate or aggravate him. I could humbly ask the Lord for forgiveness and pray for strength and courage to change my ways.

I could explore with God the question of why I let my spouse get under my skin. Why do I lose my cool with him? Is there something within me that I could change so that I don't lose it when I'm around him?

I might want to explore with the Lord how I spend my time. Do I need a little more time away from him, giving myself a little more breathing room? Or, would it help to plan *more* quality time with him by doing some activity that we both enjoy?

I may want to reflect on my unspoken expectations of marriage. Sometimes, I find myself getting frustrated with a person because I subconsciously and unrealistically try to get that person to fill a need for me that simply cannot be filled by him at this time. In my prayer then, I may want to spell out for myself exactly what an ideal spouse would be like. After doing so, I ask myself, "What needs would this ideal spouse fill for me?" Then, I consider which of these needs my real spouse might realistically be able to provide and which seem to be beyond his capacity. Of the needs I feel he could handle, I now must explore healthy ways to express those needs to him. Of the needs he can't handle right now, I must explore other healthy avenues of having those needs met.

Finally, I always return to gratitude, I praise God for the gift of my spouse and ask God to make me worthy of such a wondrous gift.

SUGGESTED SCRIPTURE PASSAGES

GENESIS 1:26–31: Male and female he created them
TOBIT 8:4–8: Tobias's marriage prayer
SONG OF SOLOMON: The entire book is a love poem
MATTHEW 7:24–27: Build on a solid foundation
MATTHEW 19:1–9: Against divorce
JOHN 15:12–16: No greater love than to give up one's life
1 CORINTHIANS 12:31—13:13: Love is…
EPHESIANS 4:25–32: Be kind, watch your words
EPHESIANS 5:22–33: Husbands, love your wives
COLOSSIANS 3:12–17: Clothe yourselves in love
1 JOHN 4:7–12: As long as we love one another,
God will live in us

PRAYER POINTERS

I pull out my old scrapbooks and photos from early in the marriage. I prayerfully peruse them, asking God to take me back through the years so that I might relive the memories of the wonderful moments in my marriage. I praise God for those moments.

I scheme with Jesus ways of letting my spouse know of my love. I try to come up with some new and creative ways. They don't have to be extravagant or even romantic as long as they are sincere.

I spend time simply praying for my spouse, praising God for all of the good things in his life, begging God on his behalf for the areas where he needs help.

In prayer I examine some of the past few conversations I've had with my spouse. I ask God to show me where I could have done a better job of communicating and how I could have been more loving.

If I'm going through a difficult time with my spouse, I simply have a conversation with God about that. I ask God to help me to the root of my anger, frustration and so on. I stay open to learn new insights about what's at the heart of the problem.

I prayerfully consider what my needs are right now. Do I need a little more private time right now? Or do I need to spend more time with my spouse? Do I need something from my spouse that he or she simply can't provide right now? If so, how can I healthily get those needs met?

I end as I began, with a prayer of gratitude for the wondrous gift of marriage and for the wondrous person of my spouse.

RELATED ENTRIES

Angry, Blew Up, Family, Forgive, Grateful

WORDS TO TAKE WITH YOU

My marriage has problems…cuz I'm in it!
—Pam Stenzel

Perfect love is the most beautiful of frustrations.
—Charlie Chaplin

The chooser's happiness lies in his congruence
with the chosen.
—Dag Hammarskjöld

A friend is one who sees you as you wish you were—
and likes you as you really are.
—Robin St. John

He who would do good to others must do it in minute
particulars; "General Good" is the plea of the
scoundrel, hypocrite and flatterer.
—William Blake

MARRIAGE

GOD, THIS MINISTRY STUFF IS TOUGH

What then is Apollos? What is Paul? Servants through whom you came to believe, as the Lord assigned to each. I planted, Apollos watered, but God gave the growth. So neither the one who plants nor the one who waters is anything, but only God who gives the growth.
—1 Corinthians 3:5–7

For a while, I was addicted to a pop song by Five for Fighting called "Superman (It's Not Easy)." In it, Superman sings about his difficult life and his existential angst. He confesses that he's always been afraid of flying and hates to do it. At the time that I was regularly listening to the song, I was feeling a bit overwhelmed by my work as a priest and a teacher and was praying a lot about that. I remember in prayer one day the song came back to mind and I snippily told Jesus, "I'm not Superman, you know." In my imagination (which is usually how Jesus speaks to me), Jesus snapped back, "Mark, who the heck asked you to be Superman? Nobody's asking you to be Superman! I'm asking you to be like me, and I was definitely *not* Superman. Superman saves through strength. I save through weakness."

It's incredible how often this issue—my childish attempt to be the savior of humankind—comes up in my prayer. Usually, Jesus patiently teases me about it and says with furrowed eyebrows, "Thank you for offering, Mark, but that position is already filled." I sheepishly smile and say, "Thank God!" Or Jesus will jokingly ask, "Mark, would you mind if I sat on the throne a while?" "Well, OK," I joke back, "but only for a little while." I'm lucky he has a sense of humor about it!

I am slowly learning the lesson, though. When I was younger, I would often agonize and get stressed out when I felt unable to fix some problem a student shared with me. Nowadays, I more often remember that "the job is already filled," and just relax about it. Over the years, I've slowly learned that the true Savior will fix the problem in his own good time. My job is simply to be open and ready to be *one* (and only one!) of the many tools in his toolbox. Earlier, during these scenarios, I would ask myself nervously, "How could I fix this problem?" Now, with great gratitude, I find myself thanking God for allowing me to play a small role in this person's life and asking God to help me to discern exactly what that small part might be. Am I to be a planter? A waterer? A weeder? A reaper? Chances are I'm only called to be one of these.

The issue is really about trust, isn't it? It's about trust that God will care for his children in his own good time, which often does not correspond to my panic-driven timetable. If I pray for that trust, I won't get so overwhelmed with my ministry. Or should I say "*His* ministry"?

SUGGESTED SCRIPTURE PASSAGES

EXODUS 33:7–17: The Lord to Moses:
"You are my intimate friend"
JEREMIAH 1:4–10: Do not say, "I am only a boy"
MATTHEW 9:35–38: Workers are few
MATTHEW 10: Jesus sending out disciples
MATTHEW 28:16–20: The great commission
JOHN 13:1–20: Jesus washes his disciples' feet
1 CORINTHIANS 3:5–7: Some plant seeds, others water,
God provides the growth
1 CORINTHIANS 12:4–31: We have different gifts
2 CORINTHIANS 4:1–15: We carry in our bodies
the dying of Jesus
2 CORINTHIANS 5:16–20: We are ambassadors of Christ
EPHESIANS 4:1–16: Lead a life worthy of the calling
PHILIPPIANS 3:7–16: I count all else as rubbish

2 TIMOTHY 1:6–14: Rekindle the gift given you
through the laying on of hands
2 TIMOTHY 4:1–8: I have run the good race…
now my crown awaits
TITUS 2:1—3:11: Teach what is consistent with sound doctrine

PRAYER POINTERS

I turn my work back over to God. In my imagination I carry my work to the altar and place it there, asking God to take it and bless it and make it holy. I acknowledge before God that this is truly God's work, not mine, and I thank God for allowing me to play a small role in it.

Using a mantra, I prayerfully turn over the most difficult part of the work to God. For example, if dealing with Billy Thomson is difficult, I chant, aloud or in my mind, over and over: "Billy is yours, Lord.…Billy is yours, Lord.…Billy is yours, Lord." If the paperwork is overwhelming, I chant, "This paperwork is yours, Lord.…This paperwork is yours.…"

I pray over the reasons why I'm feeling burned out right now. Am I trying to do more than I'm actually called to do? Have I placed my own agenda above God's? Is there some part of the job God is asking me to let go of? Do I need a break? Do I need a confidant in whom I can vent and seek advice?

In my prayerful imagination, I go back to the roots of the particular ministry in which I'm currently working. When did God first call me to this work? What is it that excited me about this ministry? I go back to the joyful moment of my discernment when I realized that God had chosen me for this work. If the Spirit moves me to do so, I allow God to call me to it again, today.

I prayerfully consider the reasons this work is of God. How does my work promote the kingdom of God? I zero in on one particular person who has been affected by my work. I ask the

MINISTRY

Lord to keep this person in the forefront of my mind today as a reminder of why I do what I do.

RELATED ENTRIES

Angry at You, Busy, Evening, Morning, Noontime, Stressed, Weary

WORDS TO TAKE WITH YOU

It's your church, Lord, I'm going to bed.
—Nighttime prayer of Blessed John XXIII

God gets the most unlikely to do the most unexpected.
—Albert E. Cliffe, *Letting Go, Letting God*

Today, I've resigned as Master of the Universe.
—Fred Crowe, s.j. (paraphrased)

MINISTRY

GOD, IT'S MORNING

> Awake, O harp and lyre!
>   I will awake the dawn.
> I will give thanks to you, O LORD, among the peoples,
>   and I will sing praises to you among the nations.
> For your steadfast love is higher than the heavens,
>   and your faithfulness reaches to the clouds.
> Be exalted, O God, above the heavens,
>   and let your glory be over all the earth.
> —Psalm 108:2–5

It's Saturday morning, and Dad, in undershirt and boxers, and I, in PJs, are lathering our faces with shaving cream as we look at ourselves in the bathroom mirror. I, being only six years old, stand on the countertop and move Dad's comb down my cheeks, pushing off the foam in rows in the same manner as my Dad's reflection is doing with his razor. I love this ritual. I love the feel of my Dad's smooth cheeks after the stubble of the night is swiped away. At some point during this father-son ceremony, Dad nods toward the rectangular sticker with the face of Jesus that is stuck to the lower-right-hand side of the mirror. My reading skills being new, I try as best I can to follow along as Dad recites the Morning Offering, "O Jesus, through the Immaculate Heart of Mary, I offer you my prayers, works, joys and sufferings of this day...."

My Saturday morning prayer times these days have the same feel as those of my childhood memories. I, in robe and slippers, sit with a cup of coffee while the Father and I prayerfully swipe away the stubble—the worries and concerns I took to bed with me the night before. Last night they kept me up and led me to believe they would soon grow out of control. But this morning I see that my Father and I can easily control them—can keep my soul smooth despite their presence. Last night as I tossed and turned in bed, the waters of chaos crashed upon the craggy rocks of my worried heart. But this morning God's breath makes everything still and quiet. And at the end of the ceremony, I offer my own Morning Offering. It's a little different from Dad's, but it serves the same purpose: it consecrates my day to the Lord.

> Eternal Word,
> Only begotten Son of the Father,
> Teach me true generosity.
> Teach me to serve as you deserve:
> To give without counting the cost.
> To fight, heedless of the wounds,
> To labor without seeking rest,
> To sacrifice myself without the thought
> of any reward,
> Except for the knowledge that I have done your will.
> Amen.
> —attributed to Saint Ignatius Loyola

SUGGESTED SCRIPTURE PASSAGES

GENESIS 1:1—2:4: The creation story
GENESIS 9:1–17: God's covenant with Noah
PSALM 65: Where morning dawns and evening fades
PSALM 92:1–5: I proclaim your love in the morning
PSALM 95:1–7: Come, and worship the Lord
PSALM 108:1–7: Arise, I will awake the dawn
ISAIAH 26:1–9: Open the gates that the
righteous nation may enter
ISAIAH 55:1–6: Seek the Lord while he may be found
LAMENTATIONS 3:22–24: Each morning you renew your graces
JOHN 21:1–14: Morning fish fry with the resurrected Jesus
ROMANS 8:26–39: What can separate us from
the love of Christ?

PRAYER POINTERS

I consider the worries that kept me up last night. I see how small they are in the light of this day. I praise God for helping me to put things in proper perspective.

I find my own favorite morning offering. I can use a popular version from a prayer book, or I could compose my own. I make it a daily ritual to pray this prayer.

While pledging to give all that I am to God's will this day, I offer everything: my work, my family, my life, back to God. I place it all under God's care.

RELATED ENTRIES

Awe, Content, Ministry, Proud, Single, Can't Wait

WORDS TO TAKE WITH YOU

Smiling, sincere, incorruptible—
His body disciplined and limber.
A man who became what he could,
And was what he was—
Ready at any moment to gather everything
Into one simple sacrifice.
—Dag Hammarskjöld

The Rabbi Zusya said a short time before his death, "In the world to come, I shall not be asked, 'Why were you not Moses?' Instead, I shall be asked, 'Why were you not Zusya?'"
—Martin Buber

MORNING

GOD, IT'S NIGHTTIME

You who live in the shelter of the Most High,
    who abide in the shadow of the Almighty,
will say to the LORD, "My refuge and my fortress;
    my God, in whom I trust."
For he will deliver you from the snare of the fowler
    and from the deadly pestilence;
he will cover you with his pinions,
    and under his wings you will find refuge;
    his faithfulness is a shield and buckler.
You will not fear the terror of the night.
—Psalm 91:1–5

So, I'm a little kid and I'm turning the big round channel dial on our old Quasar TV when I land on *The Exorcist*. It's not long before Dad notices and makes me stop watching. But I have already seen enough of it to scare the wits out of me. That night my brother and I are in bed about to fall asleep. When we finally quiet down, we hear a very strange sound in the room, "*Rowllmmm...rowlllmmm...rowllmmm.*" Well, I don't remember even touching the floor as I race out of the room to grab Dad. We go back into the room together. Now, you won't believe this but Dad flips on the light switch of my bedroom and nothing happens! The light bulb has burned out! By now, I'm just assuming that we're not going to get out of this one alive. Dad calmly grabs a flashlight and enters the room with me close behind, scared as Scooby-Doo. Sure enough the low, moaning sound continues. Dad follows it to a pile of books and toys. He digs through it until he finds the culprit: a noisy old tape recorder. It seems that by pure coincidence the corner of one of the books that were tossed on top of it as we tidied up the room before hitting the sack had fallen on the play button!

Nighttime can be a scary time. Deep in our subconscious, we wonder what is in the room that we cannot see. Even sleep itself requires that we let go of our illusion that we are consciously

NIGHTTIME

keeping our bodies alive. We teach our children to say to God, "If I should die before I wake…" knowing that when we slip into the unconsciousness of sleep tonight, we may never return.

Prayer at night, then, can be a graced opportunity to surrender our whole selves and our whole lives to the Lord. It's the time that we put our game pieces away and say goodnight to God and to all of God's creation. One who is afraid of the night will not relinquish his spirit to it. He will clutch tightly to his consciousness and remain awake and wary. But a baby, deeply asleep in the arms of his mother, is the most trusting person in the world. He completely surrenders to the protection that Mom provides and trusts that she will not let anything bad happen to him. This is how we should dispose ourselves in the arms of the God of darkness and night.

Now I lay me down to sleep,
I pray the Lord
my soul to keep.
And if I should die
before I wake,
I pray the Lord
My soul to take…

SUGGESTED SCRIPTURE PASSAGES

PSALM 16: Even at night, the Lord directs my heart
PSALM 23: The Lord is my shepherd
PSALM 43: Send out your light
PSALM 63:1–9: All through the night I will meditate on you
PSALM 121: He who keeps you will not slumber
PSALM 130:5–7: I wait for the Lord more than
watchmen for the daybreak
PSALM 131: O Lord, my soul is still
PSALM 143:1–11: In the morning let me know your love
ISAIAH 45:1–8: Treasures out of the darkness
LUKE 2:25–32: Lord, let your servant go in peace

ROMANS 8:28–39: All things work together for the good
EPHESIANS 4:26–27: The sun must not go down on your wrath
REVELATION 22:1–5: Night shall be no more

PRAYER POINTERS

One by one, I prayerfully give over all of the concerns of my day to God. I imagine each one floating out of my body, through the ceiling and up to heaven.

Without fear, I place my whole life in God's hands. From night prayer in the Liturgy of the Hours, I join hundreds of thousands of other Christians around the world as I pray with them: "May almighty God grant me a restful night and a peaceful death."

Isaiah 66:13 and Psalm 131 portray God as a mother comforting and nursing her child. In my prayerful imagination, I imagine myself as a little baby asleep in the arms of God, my mother. I allow myself to rest in that image awhile.

RELATED ENTRIES

Afraid, Despair, Lost, Parenting, Quiet, Sexually Aroused,
Worried

WORDS TO TAKE WITH YOU

Sometimes the Lord calms the storm—sometimes he lets the
storm rage and calms his child.
—Anonymous

After dark all cats are leopards.
—Zuni Proverb

Every evening I turn my worries over to God. He's going to be
up all night anyway.
—Mary C. Crowley, *Be Somebody*

NIGHTTIME

GOD, IT'S NOONTIME

> But I call upon God,
>   and the LORD will save me.
> Evening and morning and at noon
>   I utter my complaint and moan,
>   and he will hear my voice.
> He will redeem me....
> —Psalm 55:16–18

It's noon on a Wednesday very near the end of the school year, and I'm walking through the cafeteria with my lunch in hand. I'm not on lunch duty today, but the kids have been unusually mischievous in the cafeteria lately, and for some reason there's no teacher around. So I dutifully stand at one end of the large room full of loud, sloppy boys and eat my chicken basket next to the trashcan in the aisle between two long rows of tables. I'm not in a good mood today and am resenting the fact that during my first small break of the day, I have to watch these little animals as they stuff food in their mouths or throw it at each other.

Suddenly, I notice the chatter level in the room has dropped dramatically and all are excitedly glancing from me to something over my shoulder at the other end of the room. I turn around to see the microwave oven going nuts. There are sparks everywhere and a flame in the middle of the inside of the box. It is making angry, beastly sounds as though it were a trapped wildcat ready to pounce. With a mouth full of food, I start to shout to someone to unplug the thing, but then stop myself because I'm afraid the kid will electrocute himself. So I dash down the long room, run over to the wall and kick the plug out of the outlet, hoping my Texas boots are as protective as they look. Once the thing is dead, I look inside and see that someone has placed only one object inside it: an unopened, metallic pack of ketchup. Its little flame quickly goes out as I turn around to face my hundreds of amused ruffians.

It's only noon, but already it's been a long day.

Recently, at a conference for Jesuits, Father Nick Schiro, S.J., spoke about what it's like to grow old in the Society of Jesus. "In my older years, I've come to see prayer more as a mood than a time period," he said. I was struck by those words. I realized that I still have a ways to go in making my daily life prayerful rather than simply including a little prayer in my daily life. Looking back on my story of the fiery microwave, there was no part of my school day—not before walking into the cafeteria, not during my time in there and not afterward either—that I was in a prayerful state of being, a prayerful mood. Unlike another Jesuit friend of mine, who finds himself praying for his students while monitoring the cafeteria, I simply stewed that day about my deprived lunch break. I long for the day when even in the noontime of a crazy day, my spirit is in the mood of prayer.

SUGGESTED SCRIPTURE PASSAGES

PSALM 104: Praise the Lord, O my soul

PSALM 121: By day the sun shall not smite you

PSALM 122: I rejoiced when they said, "Let us go to God's house"

PSALM 127:1–2: If the Lord does not build a house

ROMANS 8:28–39: All things work together for the good

1 THESSALONIANS 5:16–18: Never cease praying

PRAYER POINTERS

I prayerfully devise ways of keeping myself in a prayerful mood throughout the day. I take a famous quote or Bible passage and write it on a small strip of paper. I place that paper in my front pocket and pull it out every so often during the day to read it over and over. I might write that line on a sticky note and

NOONTIME

attach it to my computer monitor, my car dashboard, my kitchen window.

I try to find points in my day that I can begin to make more prayerful. For example, I turn off the car radio for a few minutes each day of my commute. I spend an extra minute reflecting on my day at my Grace Before Meals. I use the times I must wait in line, in a waiting room, at a subway stop and so on, as time for me to pray the rosary or some other quiet, simple prayer.

RELATED ENTRIES

Busy, Ministry, Parenting, Quiet, Stressed

WORDS TO TAKE WITH YOU

Live in the here and now, and you will be there, then.
—A Trappist proverb

In my older years, I've come to see prayer more
as a mood than a time period.
—Nick Schiro, s.j.

A person who is nice to you, but rude to the waiter,
is not a nice person.
—Dave Barry

GOD, THIS PARENTING STUFF IS TOUGH

> After these things God tested Abraham. He said to him, "Abraham!" And he said, "Here I am." He said, "Take your son, your only son Isaac, whom you love, and go to the land of Moriah, and offer him there."
> —Genesis 22:1–2

The story of Abraham being asked to sacrifice his only son is no longer politically correct. Its image of God is too harsh and sadistic for our post-modern sensitivities. But from the standpoint of prayer, this is still an important passage on which to meditate. Why? From my observation as an outsider to parenthood, it seems that God asks parents to give up their children *every day*. When I observe my brother having to lovingly discipline his four-year-old knowing that he's got to be "the bad guy" for a while, I hear my brother answering God's call to give him up. When I observe the mother of one of my teenaged students having to stand by and watch as her son has to deal with the consequences of a bad choice made at school, I hear her painfully saying, "Yes," to God's call to give him up. When I watch my friend Cyndi worry about her college-aged daughter going off to Guatemala on a mission trip, I hear her giving in to God's command that she let her go. On the first day of kindergarten and the first day of high school, I hear God gently but firmly saying, "Give them up!" On the football field and the musical stage, at the driver's license bureau and at the prom, I hear parents willingly answer, "OK, Lord, this child is yours." At weddings, I watch as fathers give away their daughters not only in the aisle, but in their hearts, too. At the birth of grandchildren, I see older moms silently allowing their sons to care for their own babies in their own way. And late in their lives, I see elderly dads giving in when their daughters say, "Dad, let me do that for you."

PARENTING

And we say God wouldn't ask a parent to give up his child? God asks every day.

> Your children are not your children.
> They are the sons and daughters of Life's longing for itself.
> They come through you but not from you,
> And though they are with you yet they belong not to you.
> You may give them your love but not your thoughts.
> They have their own thoughts.
> You may house their bodies but not their souls,
> For their souls dwell in the house of tomorrow...
> —Kahlil Gibran

SUGGESTED SCRIPTURE PASSAGES

GENESIS 22:1–18: Sacrifice of Isaac
GENESIS 37:1–4: Jacob's love for Joseph
PSALM 127:3–5: Children are a gift from the Lord
MATTHEW 1—2: Matthew's Nativity stories
MATTHEW 15:21–28: Samaritan woman pleads for daughter
MARK 10:13–16: Bring the children to me
MARK 10:35–45: The ambition of Zebedee's sons
LUKE 1—2: Luke's Nativity stories
LUKE 2:25–35: A sword will pierce your soul
LUKE 2:41–52: Finding the boy Jesus in the Temple
LUKE 8:19–21: Your mother is here
JOHN 19:25–27: Mary at the cross
EPHESIANS 6:1–4: Children, obey your parents
COLOSSIANS 3:20–21: Don't nag your children

PRAYER POINTERS

I spend a long time, perhaps my whole prayer time, simply praising God for the wonderful gift of this child. I wonder at

PARENTING

God's love for me and faith in me. How could God entrust me with such a precious gift of his?

I recognize and acknowledge that I will never be the perfect parent. I hear God tell me, "That's really OK." I turn over my parenting, its failures and successes, to God.

I prayerfully explore what is the toughest part of parenting for me right now. I then ask myself what grace from God is needed for me to handle this (for example, patience, wisdom, perseverance, courage, humility). I spend a while begging God for the grace I need to be the parent I'm called to be.

I close my prayer as I opened it, praising God for the wonder of my vocation as parent.

RELATED ENTRIES

Blew Up, Family, Marriage, Noontime, Weary, Worried

WORDS TO TAKE WITH YOU

Nobody will ever remain faithful in a marriage, a vocation, a friendship, a family, a job, or just to his or her own integrity without sometimes sweating blood in a garden.
—Ronald Rolheiser, *The Holy Longing*

PARENTING

GOD, I'M A LAZY PROCRASTINATOR

Anyone unwilling to work should not eat. For we hear that some of you are living in idleness, mere busybodies, not doing any work. Now such persons we command and exhort in the Lord Jesus Christ to do their work quietly and to earn their own living.
—2 Thessalonians 3:10–12

During finals week at Strake Jesuit Prep at the mailboxes, I commiserated with a fellow teacher who, like me, had a large stack of not-yet-graded exams. "Yeah, it's terrible," he said, "but at least my wife loves it." "Why is that?" I asked, perplexed. "Because it's the only time I ever get anything done around the house. Only when I have a large stack of essays to grade am I motivated to clean out the garage and trim the hedges." I knew exactly what he meant. I remember once hiding away at a friend's camp in the hill country of Texas in order to do some writing. It was the perfect place: No one knew the phone number, I had no easy access to the Internet, and no friends to call up for dinner or a movie. But there was one distraction that nearly got the best of me...the television! Normally, I don't watch much television, but out there, as my laptop whirred dejectedly in the next room, I became entranced with the eating habits of the Komodo Dragon on the Discovery Channel and I just had to check CNN periodically to see if the latest Harry Potter book was selling as well as expected. Oh, and look what's on FOX: *M.A.S.H.*! I love *M.A.S.H.*!

When I pray about my procrastination, I start by just laughing at myself a bit. "Why'd you make us such funny creatures?" I ask the Lord. He just chuckles back, it seems. But placing my sluggishness before God this way seems to help a bit. Then, I ask God to help me to regard work as Pope John Paul II regards it:

> By enduring the toil of work in union with Christ crucified for us, man in a way collaborates with the Son of God for the redemption of humanity. He shows himself a true disciple of Christ by carrying the cross in his turn every day in the activity that he is called upon to perform.... (*Laborem exercens*)

I need to view work—whether it be ministering, parenting or answering phones at a receptionist desk—as a vocation from God. Ultimately, God wants me to work with him to create a new heaven and a new earth. Humankind should know the place that his or her work has, says the pope, "not only in *earthly progress* but also in *the development of the Kingdom of God*." What an awesome calling! God's great love has allowed *me*—with all of my laziness and procrastination, my sins and setbacks, my faults and failures—to play a role in his salvific plan. Of all the ways that God could have chosen to save the world, God chose a way that would make me his coworker. And this is no less true of jobs that are not ministry-specific; all forms of honest labor participate in the ever-evolving city of God.

"Whom shall I send?" God asks me. *M.A.S.H.* will have to wait. I have work to do.

SUGGESTED SCRIPTURE PASSAGES

1 SAMUEL 3:1–10: Here I am, Lord
PSALM 127:1–2: If the Lord does not build a house
PROVERB 6:6–9: Look to the ant, you lazybones!
MATTHEW 9:35–38: The harvest is plenty, laborers are few
MATTHEW 10:1–20: Jesus sending out the disciples
MATTHEW 11:28–30: Come to me all you who are weary
MATTHEW 28:16–20: Go, make disciples of all nations
LUKE 9:57–62: Keep your hand to the plow
LUKE 17:7–10: Master says to the servant: "Fix my dinner"

2 CORINTHIANS 9:5–7: The one who sows generously
will reap generously
EPHESIANS 6:10–17: Do all that your duty requires
COLOSSIANS 3:22–25: Be slaves of Christ
2 THESSALONIANS 3:6–15: He who does not work should not eat
HEBREWS 12:11–13: Strengthen the weak hand
and feeble knees
REVELATION 3:15–22: Against being lukewarm

PRAYER POINTERS

I read the pope's words from the preceding reflection again and again, pondering the value of honest labor. I turn to my task at hand and ask God to show me how it is that this particular task, however menial, is a part of God's divine plan.

I listen for God's invitation for me to take up my cross and follow him in doing this work. I listen for a response from me back to God.

I begin my work with a little prayer to remind myself that honest labor is the work of God. I put some symbol of my connection with God nearby, for example, a lighted candle or a small crucifix. I ask God to make my work hour a holy hour, one that I treat with the reverence and respect it deserves.

I reflect on all of the unemployed and the psychologically or physically unemployable people of the world. In this light, I praise God for giving me the task at hand. I ask God to help me never to take my work for granted. If I work with my hands, I praise God for the gift of those hands. If my work requires a lot of complex thought, I praise God for the gift of my intelligence. In this way, I consider all the gifts I've been given for the task at hand, and I praise God for the privilege of being able to use each of them and all of them together.

RELATED ENTRIES

Busy, Confront, Habits, Hate, Morning, Weary

WORDS TO TAKE WITH YOU

We act as though comforts and luxury were the chief require-
ments of life, when all we need to make us really happy is
something to be enthusiastic about.
—Charles Kingsley

Fear not that your life will have an end. Fear that it will have
no beginning.
—Cardinal Newman

To love what you do and feel that it matters—
how could anything be more fun?
—Katherine Graham

PROCRASTINATOR

GOD, I'M PROUD OF MYSELF

> I give thanks to my God always for you because of the grace of God that has been given you in Christ Jesus, for in every way you have been enriched in him in speech and knowledge of every kind—just as the testimony of Christ has been strengthened among you—so that you are not lacking in any spiritual gift....
> —1 Corinthians 1:4–7

A persistent fallacy that has haunted Christianity almost since its inception is the belief that I, as a Christian, am called to be self-effacing and self-loathing—that I should deny any positive traits or qualities which others might try to pin on me. If anyone pays me a compliment, I should work hard to prove to that person that I really don't deserve to be complimented, that I really didn't do anything special, that someone else should be the one complimented. The belief is that I should always think badly of myself and degrade myself in front of others. Some even believe that this is the essence of Christianity.

Nothing could be further from the truth! We Christians, of all people, should take great delight in who we are and in the good things we accomplish, knowing full well that God is taking delight in us. "God looked at everything he had made, and he found it very good," says the Book of Genesis. If God calls me the precious apple of his eye, is it right for me to argue? If I insult the work of art, am I not insulting the artist?

God takes delight in me as a mother delights in the beauty and goodness of her child, and my beauty and goodness only grow when I joyfully delight in myself. Teresa of Avila defines humility as "honesty in the face of God." Ironically, a prayerful acknowledgment of my goodness will lead not to sinful pride but to joy and humility. I become awestruck by how good God has been to me by gifting me so abundantly. This joy, humility and awe make puffing myself up through self-flattery unnecessary. Sinful pride, on the other hand, begins with an unconscious, unacknowledged *poor self-image*. Because I think poorly of myself, I have to build myself up by cutting others down; this leads to being prideful and judgmental.

My prayer, then, should be a joyous celebration of the wondrous creation that is me. Only then will I appreciate and understand my gifts enough to share them with those whom I am called to serve. A wedding is a great example of this. Weddings are celebrated when a couple says to the community, "Look at what a great gift we've discovered in ourselves!" and the community shouts back, "Yes, God is present in you!" It is through this acknowledgment, affirmation and celebration that we allow the marriage to be Christ's saving presence in our world. Likewise, in prayerfully acknowledging, affirming and celebrating my gifts, I lift the bushel basket and allow my Christ-light to dispel a little of the darkness of the world.

SUGGESTED SCRIPTURE PASSAGES

GENESIS 1—2:4: Creation: It is good!
DEUTERONOMY 32:9–14: The apple of God's eye
PSALM 139: I praise you that I am wonderfully made
ISAIAH 43:1–8: When you walk through fire,
you shall not be burned
MATTHEW 5:13–16: Let your light shine
LUKE 10:17–20: The disciples return jubilant
LUKE 18:28–30: For leaving everything, you will receive one
hundred-fold
LUKE 24:13–35: Were not our hearts burning within us?
1 CORINTHIANS 1:1–9: You are not lacking in any spiritual gift
2 CORINTHIANS 9: Paul praises their generosity
2 TIMOTHY 4:1–8: I have run the good race...now my crown
awaits

PROUD OF MYSELF

PRAYER POINTERS

As an actor allows herself the pleasure of basking in the success of a good performance, so I allow myself to sit with God and bask in the joy of having done something well. All the while, with great humility, I stand in awe of the Creator who led me to this point. I praise him in wonder for inviting me to this vocation and for granting me the gifts to fulfill it.

I contentedly relive the experience, this time specifically searching for God's presence in the experience. Where was God in this? How was God's glory manifested?

Saint Ignatius Loyola says, "When in consolation, prepare for desolation." I do so by acknowledging before God and before my loved ones that God is truly present and active in my life. I may even want to set it down in my journal. This way, when I'm going through dark times in the future, I'll have reminders that this calling of mine is not merely an illusion.

RELATED ENTRIES

Content, Evening, Grateful, Joyful, Ministry, Morning,
Sinfully Proud

WORDS TO TAKE WITH YOU

It is amazing what one can do when one
doesn't know what one can't do.
—Garfield the Cat

GOD, I'M SINFULLY PROUD

I have applied all this to Apollos and myself for your benefit, brothers and sisters, so that you may learn through us the meaning of the saying, "Nothing beyond what is written," so that none of you may be puffed up in favor of one against another. For who sees anything different in you? What do you have that you did not receive? And if you received it, why do you boast as if it were not a gift?
—1 Corinthians 4:6–7

The summer before my ordination to the priesthood, I made my annual retreat in the wooded village of Weston, Massachusetts. One of my concerns was my own lifetime struggle with pride. At various times in my life, I've been distressed by my holier-than-thou attitude and have had to beg the Lord for the grace of humility. Often, the clergy are placed on a pedestal as though they were sacred objects themselves. I've seen many a priest poisoned by this praise and affirmation. Many become "puffed up," to use Saint Paul's words. So, on this retreat not long before my ordination, I asked the Lord to tell me how I might avoid becoming puffed up and prideful. Several days went by in which the Lord chose other topics to discuss with me and skirted my question about pride.

On this particular retreat, I used Mark's Gospel as my guide and day by day followed Jesus from his baptism in the first chapter of Mark to his Resurrection in the last. All was going well until about three fifths of the way through. Jesus was fast approaching his death and was going through Jericho on the way to Jerusalem. At the wall of the city gate, he encountered the blind man Bartimaeus crying out, "Jesus, Son of David, have mercy on me" (see Mark 10:46–52). In my prayer I imagined myself as that blind beggar and experienced Jesus' healing touch. But in the next prayer time, as Jesus went into the city, I, in my imagination, found myself back against the city wall, blind and outside the loop. I begged Jesus again to have mercy

PROUD

and to let me accompany him. Days went by, and Jesus passed from Jericho to Jerusalem and on to his death and burial, and all the while I was stuck at the city wall, begging for mercy. I kept asking Jesus why would he want me to pray as a beggar for so long. Why wouldn't he let me move on from there? Come to think of it, doesn't Jesus just give his mercy as a free gift? Do I really have to beg for it?

Very late in the retreat, Jesus brought me understanding. In my imagination, he said something to this effect, "Mark, you asked me for help with your pride and I have answered your prayer. I have made you a blind beggar desperately pleading for salvation. Of course, I grant salvation freely and need no begging from you. But you need to beg, Mark. Only then will you remember that salvation is a gift from me and has nothing to do with how good are your homilies or how well you handle a tricky confession. You need to beg me for mercy, Mark, and you need do so all your life."

And so, from then on, and particularly when I find myself puffed up with pride, I go back to the walls of Jericho, begging Jesus for mercy.

Jesus, Son of David, have mercy on me, a sinner.

SUGGESTED SCRIPTURE PASSAGES

MATTHEW 18:1–5: Who is the greatest?
MATTHEW 19:16–30: The rich young man
MATTHEW 23: Hypocrisy of the Pharisees
MARK 10:46–52: The blind man Bartimaeus
LUKE 17:7–10: Master says to the servant: "Fix my dinner"
LUKE 18:9–14: The publican and the Pharisee
JOHN 9: The smug Pharisees are blind
JOHN 13:1–20: Jesus washes his disciples' feet
ROMANS 12: Do not think of yourself more highly than you ought

PROUD

1 CORINTHIANS 4:6–8: So that you don't become "puffed up"

2 CORINTHIANS 12:7–10: My grace is sufficient for you

PRAYER POINTERS

Most importantly, I acknowledge my pride before God. I stare squarely into the face of my pride and call it by its name: sin. I recognize that this is the evil spirit's way of trying to steal a victory from the Lord's effective work in my life.

I pray over Mark 10:46–52. I imagine myself as the blind Bartimaeus. I use his prayer as my mantra, "Jesus, Son of David, have mercy on me, a sinner."

I go to the sacrament of reconciliation. It is always humbling to have to say to another person that I am a prideful man.

I ponder the fact that pride is actually a manifestation of a low self-esteem. People who have a strong self-esteem have no need of puffing themselves up. I ask God to show me how I am still in need of his healing grace. I ask God to help me to face the part of myself that *needs* to be built up. I ask God to lift me up in those areas so that I won't have to foolishly prop myself up.

I ask God to show me ways that I might build up the people around me. How might I help others to shine without denying my own goodness?

RELATED ENTRIES

Guilty, Judgmental, Ministry, Proud, Sinned

WORDS TO TAKE WITH YOU

To be humble is to accept that you are full of pride.
—Anonymous
We all have to try to become holy on our own, and fail, before
we can approach God with humility.
—Mark Salzman, *Lying Awake*

PROUD

GOD, I FEEL STILL AND QUIET

> Be still, and know that I am God!
> —Psalm 46:10

My four-year-old nephew has a flair for the dramatic. On a recent camping trip with my family, I found myself responsible for quieting him down for bed one night. While lying on the couch-turned-bed in the camper, he passionately described for me several of his favorite Pokémon characters and what each "evolved" (his word!) into. At times he got so excited that he grabbed my face with his two small hands to make sure I understood the enormity of his point. Trying not to laugh, I attentively listened to him, all the while rubbing his head or his chest to make him sleepy. Before long the pauses between descriptions grew longer and eventually he fell into a contented sleep (in which his Pokémon characters came to life, I'm sure).

Sometimes I think that this must be what my relationship with God is like in my prayer. I sit there excitedly rattling off my concerns of the day, pleading for help, begging for mercy, praising his goodness, and all the while God is smiling and massaging my soul, waiting for me to get quiet and still. Like my nephew, Michael, I resist the quiet and insist on covering my chosen topics of this particular prayer time. But if I am even a little open to God's presence, I may eventually find myself drifting into a more peaceful place, as though I were floating on a still pond after a rainstorm.

Often in my prayer life, I feel called to work through some problem with God, or to sing his praises, or to *do* some other *activity* with God. But there are other times when I sense that the Lord wants me to be quiet and *know* in an experiential way that the Lord is God. I find that the more prayerful I am in any given phase of my life, the more I'm able to feel that tug toward stillness in prayer. Contemplation, as opposed to other types of prayer, specifically "looks out for" those moments. When I contemplate, I *lean into being*. That is, I lean my prayer time more toward those quiet moments than toward prayerful activities, such as the recitation of prayers. I lean, not force, my way into that place of stillness.

Sometimes these moments of stillness even occur at the busiest points of my day. In the midst of some important computer work or in the middle of a meeting I find myself getting quiet deep down. As far as I am able, I allow the Lord to take me to that quiet place. Evidently, it's what I need most at that moment. If I'm alone in the office, I might turn off the light and close the door for a few moments. Or, if there isn't time for that, I'll simply take my fingers off the keyboard and watch my fish in the aquarium, joining them in their lazy drifting.

QUIET

SUGGESTED SCRIPTURE PASSAGES

1 KINGS 19:9–13: God in the tiny, whispering wind
PSALM 46:9–12: Be still and know I am God
PSALM 131: O Lord, my soul is still
ISAIAH 30:15–21: By waiting you shall be saved;
in quiet your strength lies
MATTHEW 6:5–8: When you pray, go by yourselves
MARK 4:35–41: Jesus calms the sea
MARK 6:30–33: Come away awhile
LUKE 10:38–42: Martha, Martha, you are anxious
about many things
JOHN 1:35–39: Jesus says, "Come and see"

PRAYER POINTERS

I find a comfortable sitting position, one that is relaxing but not so much so that I will easily fall asleep. I sit quietly a few moments, allowing my breathing to slow down and my body to relax.

I close my eyes and begin to focus all of my attention on my breathing in and out. Many spiritual guides say, "Become aware of your breathing," because most of the time I don't even notice it. I observe it as though I were a scientist who has just discovered, to his astonishment the strange and wondrous act of respiration. I note that as I further relax my breathing gets slower, quieter.

I choose a word or short phrase that expresses my desire for God to be present. Some of my favorite mantras are "Jesus," "Maranatha" (or its English translation, "Come, Lord, Jesus," from Revelation 22:20), and "My Lord, My God" (from John 20:28). I also like using John Paul II's motto, "*Totus tuus*," which is Latin for "Totally yours." I begin to call on God by slowly and reverently repeating my mantra over and over in my mind.

I notice that my mantra is gradually coming in sync with my breathing. Using the word, "Jesus," for instance, as I inhale I say the syllable, "Jee," and as I exhale I say, "sus."

I continue this practice for several minutes. Over time (and it does take time), I will notice myself reaching a state of quiet.

RELATED ENTRIES

Awe, Busy, Content, Evening, Lonely, Nighttime, Noontime, Single

WORDS TO TAKE WITH YOU

When we are alone and quiet, we fear that something will be whispered into our ear, and for this reason we hate the quiet and drug ourselves with social life.
—Nietzsche

If you ever have the opportunity to keep your mouth shut,
don't pass it up.
—Jon Hassler (paraphrased)

We do not go into the desert to escape people but to learn
how to find them.
—Thomas Merton

God is no more present in a church than in a drinking bar,
but, generally, we are more present to God in a church than
in a bar.
—Sheila Cassidy, *Prayer for Pilgrims*

QUIET

GOD, I'M SAD

> Come to me, all you that are weary and are carrying heavy
> burdens, and I will give you rest. Take my yoke upon you,
> and learn from me; for I am gentle and humble in heart,
> and you will find rest for your souls. For my yoke is easy,
> and my burden is light.
> —Matthew 11:28–30

Even though we lived within the "city limits" of our small Cajun town of Church Point, Louisiana, our pet cats and dogs were not tightly bound by its leash laws; no pun intended. Like us, they were free to run and play with the neighbors. This was great from the animal's perspective, of course, but only for the short term. Living free outside meant that they had to contend with life-threatening entities. The greatest danger of all was that of getting run over by a vehicle. This is how most of my pets met their ends.

I remember well the day Mom came into the living room to give me the bad news that my latest cat had met this same fate. I don't remember his name, but I remember that he was black, white and gray and that he had a sweet disposition. I remember bursting with tears and Momma holding me. As I recall, she didn't have a lot to say; she just stood there enveloping me in her embrace. After a little while, she sat me in our green upholstered chair and brought me Oreos and milk while some cartoon was beginning on TV. It wasn't very long before I stopped whimpering and became more interested in the Oreos and in the capers of the cartoon characters.

Decades later, I was sitting in my office at Dallas Jesuit Prep grading papers when one of my fifteen-year-old students came by, ostensibly to check his grade posted on my office door. "How's it going?" I asked with a smile. "OK," he quietly replied. He finished looking at his grade but just stood there, facing the door. "Is something wrong?" I asked. He was quiet for a long moment and then with filled-up eyes he turned to me and said, "Have you ever had a cat?" But by the time he got to the word "cat," the floodgates had opened. "Come in and shut the door," I quietly told him. Through many tears the boy explained that his mom had just told him over the public phone (which is in the center of a popular spot on the campus) that his cat had to be put to sleep at the vet's. Subconsciously taking my cue from my own grief years ago, I didn't say much. I just sat with him for a while and let him cry. Obviously, he was still sad when he left my office that day, but he did feel much better having found a hiding place in the school to have a good cry.

When I'm sad, I often go to God with questions or with a request to "make it go away." Sometimes God gives me answers and sometimes my sadness almost miraculously disappears during my prayer time. But most of the time, God doesn't say much or do much. He just envelopes me in his embrace and I feel a little better afterward.

SUGGESTED SCRIPTURE PASSAGES

PSALM 6: Prayer in time of distress
PSALM 137:1–6: We sat mourning and weeping
MATTHEW 5:3–12: The Beatitudes
MATTHEW 11:28–30: Come to me all you who are weary
MATTHEW 28: Matthew's Resurrection narrative
MARK 8:34–38: Anyone who wishes to follow me
LUKE 24: Luke's Resurrection narrative
JOHN 12:23–25: Unless a grain of wheat falls to the ground
JOHN 16:33: You will suffer, but take courage
JOHN 20—21: John's Resurrection narrative
2 CORINTHIANS 4:7–18: We are struck down but not destroyed
HEBREWS 5:8–10: He learned obedience through suffering
REVELATION 21:1–5: New heavens and new earth

PRAYER POINTERS

Very often when I'm going through some negative emotion, I make myself even more miserable by trying too hard to rid myself of any bad feelings. Sometimes, the better thing to do is simply allow myself to be sad for a while. I shouldn't wallow in it, but it's OK if I'm not happy and cheerful from time to time. With this in mind, I go to prayer allowing myself to be sad today. I imagine God to be a great big strong yet infinitely gentle grandfather who places me in his lap and envelopes me in his protective and loving arms. I allow myself to cry awhile there in God's lap.

I reflect on the quote below from the Talmud. I ponder the fact that Christ's sufferings were an integral part of the salvific plan—one cannot resurrect without first dying. Trusting in God, I profess my belief that God will use my present suffering to make me a resurrected person, stronger than ever. Even if I don't feel this confidence right now, I trust that it is true.

I trust that some day I will move beyond this, and I dream of the day when I will be able to help others through a similar experience. I beg God to transform me from a wounded victim to a wounded healer of others who have the same problem. I reflect on Fleming's quote, below. I imagine this darkness I'm in to be the womb of God, and I trust that if I am patient, great things will be born soon.

RELATED ENTRIES

Dying, Grieving, Hurt, Joyful, Lost, Quiet, Weary

WORDS TO TAKE WITH YOU

With thy very wounds I will heal thee.
—*The Talmud*

When we are in darkness, we are in the womb of God.
—David Fleming, S.J.

GOD, I'M SEXUALLY AROUSED

> You are stately as a palm tree,
> and your breasts are like its clusters.
> I say I will climb the palm tree
> and lay hold of its branches.
> O may your breasts be like clusters of the vine,
> and the scent of your breath like apples,
> and your kisses like the best wine
> that goes down smoothly,
> gliding over lips and teeth.
> I am my beloved's,
> and his desire is for me.
> —Song of Solomon 7:7–10

Good Christian people often worry about their sexual feelings. They are embarrassed and ashamed of them. They see that whole area of their lives as "dirty" and "ungodly." But the church is unequivocal about this: sexuality is a gift from God, not a curse from the devil. It is holy and beautiful. Like all other gifts our sexual thoughts and feelings can be misused, of course. When we do so, we call this lust. But sexual thoughts and feelings themselves are not sinful. They are natural, biological responses to stimuli. At the scientific level, they serve the purpose of attracting us to others so that we might procreate and carry on the species. At the spiritual level, they serve to bring us to closer union with another and to give us a preview of the joy of becoming one with the Creator at the end of time. As pleasurable as the experience of sex is, how much more so must be the union we will experience in heaven! That is why the church has always used the Old Testament book the Song of Solomon, which is essentially a sensual love poem between two lovers, as a metaphor for our love from and for God. Saint Teresa of Avila, a doctor of the church and one of the most important mystics of all time, also used sexual metaphors and vocabulary to describe her relationship with God.

Our sexual thoughts and feelings, then, should not be a source of shame but a source of joy. Instead of hiding these experiences, we should share them with God and use them to remind us how great it is to be alive, how great it is to be a creature of God and how wondrously we are created (Psalm 139).

There are days, of course, when we are pestered by our sexual feelings. We try our best to move on from them, but our sexual urgings continue to distract us from going about our daily tasks. Getting angry, ashamed or frustrated seems only to exacerbate the problem. A better way to deal with these lingering thoughts and feelings is simply to laugh at them. Jesus and I can have a good laugh about how juvenile we humans can be at times, how like the animals we are. To laugh at them diffuses them, renders them powerless in their efforts to throw me off target. To laugh at them acknowledges them for what they are: merely emotions that will pass away again in a short time.

SUGGESTED SCRIPTURE PASSAGES

GENESIS 1:31—2:4: Creation story 1
GENESIS 2:4b—3:24: Creation story 2 and
the fall of humankind
GENESIS 29:9–11: Jacob admiring Rachel
2 SAMUEL 6:11–14: David dancing in procession of the ark
PSALM 139:1–18: I give thanks for I am fearfully,
wonderfully made
SONG OF SOLOMON : The entire book is a love poem
MATTHEW 13:24–30: Let the weeds grow with wheat

PRAYER POINTERS

In prayer I present the sexual side of me to God. I tell God that I've been feeling sexually aroused lately, and I allow him to ease my conscience about it. I imagine him fashioning me in my

SEXUALLY AROUSED

mother's womb (Psalm 139:13), and, with great delight (and a little mischievousness?) creating the sexual part of my personality. I see this side of myself as God sees it: a beautiful gift for uniting us to one another and to God.

I praise God for making me so alive as to get this excited. I talk to God about the people that I am aroused by. I praise God for making such physically attractive people. I recognize it as just one more way that God has created a beautiful world. I allow God to help me see some of the other gifts that this person possesses, and I thank God for each of those gifts.

I pray over the Old Testament book, the Song of Solomon. I imagine that the two lovers in the garden are God and me. Reading the poems this way, I get in touch with my burning desire to grow closer to God and God's burning desire to grow closer to me.

The Letter to the Hebrews tells us that Jesus was like us in every way but sin. If this is true, then Jesus must have felt physically attracted to others just as I do. I have a conversation with Jesus about this. I allow him to tell me about the attraction he felt for this person or that person. I ask him to show me how he celebrated his gift of sexuality without abusing the gift.

SEXUALLY AROUSED

RELATED ENTRIES

Awe, Body, Guilty, Lonely, Love, Lust, Nighttime, Single

WORDS TO TAKE WITH YOU

Take God very seriously; but don't take yourself seriously at all.
—Saint Teresa of Avila

GOD, THIS SINGLE LIFE IS TOUGH

> The word of the LORD came to me: You shall not take a wife, nor shall you have sons or daughters in this place.
> —Jeremiah 16:1–2

As a Jesuit I travel quite a bit, and as an unmarried man, I usually travel alone. In the early part of my Jesuit life, I would sometimes feel lonely in the terminals of airports. I remember watching with longing as lovers would kiss each other hello or good-bye with tremendous emotion and as families would wait with balloons, signs and big smiles for the long lost son or daughter, brother or sister, aunt or uncle. And here I was with only my bagel and *USA Today* to keep me company. As time went on, though, I grew to relish my time alone on travel days. Believe it or not, I didn't even mind multiple stops with long layovers; travel days for me had turned into times of much-needed reflection and solitude. This realization came to me one day, when I ended up traveling with a friend and felt irritated by his presence and cheated out of my seclusion!

If I am called to be single, whether for life or only for a while longer, it's important that I grow spiritually comfortable with being alone. For the married person, the experience of loneliness is often a calling to grow closer to one's spouse. For the single person, though, the experience of loneliness is usually a calling to mind the richness of aloneness—to experience the stillness of a quiet apartment and to explore the depths of one's longing for union with the Divine. The single life, then, is an opportunity for spousal intimacy with God. The single person looks to God for intimacy, companionship and generativity.

In terms of relating to the world, as the married person is called to use the gift of marriage for the sake of the kingdom, so must the single person use his status for service of one's neighbor. A married couple may be called to raise a family that seeks first the kingdom and inspires others in the world to do the same. A single person may be called to devote his time, money and energy to a Christian cause such as a church youth group, an organization that serves the poor, or even the caretaking of an elderly person or handicapped person who would otherwise be neglected. The point is this: a single person, whether single for the short-term or for life, is called to this state by God. It is a vocation, no less important or holy than the vocation to become a priest, brother or nun. The single person, then, must pray that he be made worthy of such a calling, that he be able to discern how to use this gift for God's greater glory and that he may experience God's intimate and saving love through his experience of being single.

SUGGESTED SCRIPTURE PASSAGES

PSALM 139: I praise you that I am wonderfully made.
JEREMIAH 16:1–4: Jeremiah told to be single
MATTHEW 19:10–13: Unmarried for the sake of the kingdom
LUKE 10:38–42: Martha, Martha, you are anxious
about many things
LUKE 18:28–30: Jesus, we have left everything to follow you
1 CORINTHIANS 7:8–9: Remain in the state that you're in;
don't marry
EPHESIANS 5:8–21: Make the most of the present opportunity

PRAYER POINTERS

Together with God, I go through all the great things about being single. One by one, I praise God for the joys that come from not being attached to anyone but Christ.

I prayerfully search for a model or mentor in the single state of life. In prayer I go through all of this person's qualities. How is it that she lives so well in the single state of life? In what ways does she use this gift to make her a better person? To make the world more like the kingdom of God? What behaviors or attitudes does she seem to avoid to remain healthy?

I consider the fact that Jesus was single all of his life. I see him struggling with some of the same difficulties of single life with which I struggle. I speak to him about it. I ask him the same questions I asked of my model above. I allow him to tell me all about it.

I ask God how it is that I might use my single status for his greater glory. What contributions might I make to the work of the church that a married person could not normally do? I begin to plan with Jesus ways to use my gift of the single life to further God's kingdom here on earth.

RELATED ENTRIES

Content, Hate, Lonely, Ministry, Morning, Quiet,
Sexually Aroused

WORDS TO TAKE WITH YOU

If I truly love myself, I am with someone
I like twenty-four hours a day!
—John Powell, S.J.

GOD, I'VE SINNED

Too heavy for us, our offenses, but you wipe them away.
—Psalm 65:3 (from the Liturgy of the Hours)

A couple of years ago, I learned that one of my former students from Dallas was dying of bone cancer at the tragically young age of twenty-one. I immediately sent him a letter, part of which read something like this:

> Dear Andrew,
>
> Remember me? Mr. Thibs? It's Father Thibs now!
>
> I was in Dallas this past weekend for a wedding and was told about your cancer. Andrew, I can't tell you how sorry I am to hear the news. I can't imagine the trial you've been through.
>
> Since last night I've been remembering how much fun I had teaching your sophomore theology class. I remember once telling y'all a story about how on the track field one day, I washed my hands with Gatorade because I had cheap yellow sunglasses on and thought the liquid was water. You thought that was so funny and couldn't stop laughing. You even drew a picture of me in front of the Gatorade cooler—sunglasses and all. I still laugh when I think about that picture.
>
> I remember another story about you. One day in class we had a discussion about the sacrament of reconciliation. I remember you saying something to this effect: "Mr. Thibs, I'm not sure I could do it. Yeah, I can say a bunch of my small sins. But what if there's something I'm really embarrassed about? How can I say that to the priest?" And I told you, "Yeah, I know what you mean, Andrew. That's tough to do. But imagine how it would feel to get everything off your chest—to say anything and everything embarrassing about yourself. And

then to hear this representative of Christ say, 'Your sins are forgiven.' Imagine how that might feel, Andrew."

Well, a few days later, after the school had a reconciliation service, you came to class with the biggest smile in the world and you said, "Guess what, Mr. Thibs, I did it! I confessed everything!" I asked you, "How does it feel?" Your smile got even bigger and you said, "It feels great!" I will never forget that smile.

A few days after sending off that letter, I shared that story at a youth conference in Mobile, Alabama. For the rest of the conference, these young people prayed for Andrew. Near the end of it, I was joking around with one of them and he suddenly got serious and said, "Hey, Father Thibs, you know how you told us that story about the boy who 'did it'? Well, I just wanted you to know that yesterday at the reconciliation service, I did it, too."

And you know, that kid had the same smile that Andrew had that great day several years back.

SUGGESTED SCRIPTURE PASSAGES

PSALM 51: Wash me, O Lord
PSALM 103:1–18: As far as east is from west,
so far is my sin from God
PSALM 130: If you, O Lord, should mark our guilt
ISAIAH 55:1–13: All who are thirsty, come to the water
JOEL 2:15—3:2: Call to penance; the Lord responds
LUKE 12:13–21: Against greed
LUKE 15:11–32: The Prodigal Son
LUKE 22:31–34: Jesus to Peter:
Satan seeks to sift you like wheat
LUKE 23:39–43: Jesus saves the good thief
JOHN 8:1–11: Jesus: "The one without sin, cast the first stone"

JOHN 21:15–17: Jesus forgives Peter

ROMANS 5:20–21: Where sin increases, grace abounds

PRAYER POINTERS

Instead of hiding it, I place my sinfulness before God. I tell God about every detail, leaving no part of it out. Knowing that God is love, I allow God to respond. I go to the sacrament of reconciliation and enjoy its fruits.

I pray over the passage wherein Jesus tells Peter that he will sin gravely, but that Jesus has prayed that he be strong and recover (Luke 22:31–34). I imagine Christ as knowing that I was going to sin even before I did so. I imagine Jesus praying to the Father on my behalf—praying that I might recover from this sin, that I might allow God to forgive me, and that I might allow God to use this experience as an instrument of grace for myself and for others.

I pray over George Williams's quote below. I imagine just how puny my sin is compared to the all-powerful love and mercy of God. I recognize that my unbelief that God has forgiven me is an unbelief in the infinite mercy of God and in the power of this mercy to cleanse me.

I picture God the Father as a strong, mighty man who melts when I tell him of my sin. I imagine him lifting my chin, looking me in the eye, and saying, "I forgive you and I love you." I use the Father's words to me as my mantra, again and again allowing God to say, "I forgive you and I love you," until the words begin to sink in and take root.

I ask God to show me how I might use my sinfulness and recovery to make me a better person. I consider how I might help, at least through prayer, those who struggle with this same sin.

RELATED ENTRIES

Addicted, Blew Up, Guilty, Habits, Hate, Jealous, Judgmental,
Lust, Procrastinator, Sinfully Proud

WORDS TO TAKE WITH YOU

God's love is more powerful than my sinfulness.
—George Williams, S.J.

All ordinary people think themselves extraordinary in
their sinfulness when in reality it is their simple goodness
that is extraordinary.
—Mark E. Thibodeaux, S.J.

GOD, I'M STRESSED OUT

For you yourselves know how you ought to imitate us; we were not idle when we were with you, and we did not eat anyone's bread without paying for it; but with toil and labor we worked night and day, so that we might not burden any of you. This was not because we do not have that right, but in order to give you an example to imitate.
—2 Thessalonians 3:7–9

If I am complaining to myself, to God and to others that I'm stressed out, then I basically have two choices: (1) I could lighten my load and stop complaining, or (2) I could stop complaining. To a great extent, burnout is a state of mind. I had a friend who made himself miserable by constantly reflecting on how tired he was and how burdened he felt by his job. He made those around him miserable, too! He may or may not have been too busy (those who worked with him wondered what he did all day), but one thing is clear: his preoccupation with his stress levels did nothing to alleviate the problem. It seems that the unfreedom he felt in his life did not come from outside circumstances, but from an inner disposition. I've often wondered what he would have been like if he didn't *perceive* himself to be too busy? What prompts me to ask such a question is the fact that I know others who accomplish an astounding amount of work in a given day and yet never seem to be stressed out. I have noticed the same phenomenon in my own life. My sense of feeling burdened or free at any given time has less to do with the workload itself and more to do with my own emotional state at the time.

Let's look at it from another perspective. Science tells us that a gas expands to fill the space it occupies. In the same way, the dimensions of the tasks at hand expand to fill the time allotted. In other words, my day will often feel full regardless of how much or how little I actually have to accomplish. What makes the difference is my attitude toward the day's tasks.

My own salvation from stress comes when I start enjoying the individual trees and stop fearing the huge and scary forest. Stress comes when I can't recognize the goodness of the person with whom I'm speaking because I'm too preoccupied with the tremendous work I have to accomplish by the end of the day. My salvation comes when God graces me with an appreciation for the present moment—when I experience the divine presence of Christ in the person (or even the paperwork!) before me and give that present presence the reverence it deserves. At the end of my day, I may not have accomplished all that I set out to do, but I am in touch with a God who wishes to be my savior. And so I surrender the joys and struggles, the successes and failures to that God I find in every moment, every person, every stressful task.

SUGGESTED SCRIPTURE PASSAGES

ISAIAH 30:15–21: In quiet your strength lies
MATTHEW 11:28–30: Come to me all you who are weary
MATTHEW 19:16–30: The rich young man
LUKE 6:47–49: Build your house on rock
LUKE 14:25–34: Bear your cross
LUKE 17:7–10: Master says to the servant, "Fix my dinner"
EPHESIANS 6:10–17: Do all that your duty requires
COLOSSIANS 3:22–25: Be slaves of Christ
2 CORINTHIANS 5:16–20: We are ambassadors of Christ
2 THESSALONIANS 3:10–12: He who shall not work should not eat

PRAYER POINTERS

In my prayerful imagination, I go back to various times in my life when I was extremely busy yet extremely happy. I relive that joyful busyness now. I prayerfully explore what is different between that joyful busyness then and my present stress-filled busyness. I ask God to help me see my busy life as a gift-filled life—to see that every task in my life is an opportunity to give God praise through my labor.

I pray over Matthew 11:28–30. I see that even though I am "weary and find life burdensome," Christ does not call me to sit and rest with him but to become his yoke partner, his coworker. I ask Christ to show me that my life is manageable after all— that it is my fears, anxieties and compulsions that make my work burdensome, not the work itself.

In prayer I accept Christ's offer to become his yoke-partner. I promise to give over my work and my whole life to him. I acknowledge that I am only a small part of God's immense plan of salvation, and I praise God for allowing me to be a part of that salvific plan.

STRESSED

RELATED ENTRIES

Busy, Despair, Ministry, Noontime, Procrastinator, Weary, Worried

WORDS TO TAKE WITH YOU

Better to burn out than to rust out.
—William Barclay

If I drive to work both aggressively and speedily, I eventually arrive at my office with the same manic personality that brought me here.
—James Keenan, S.J.

I want to be thoroughly used up when I die.
—George Bernard Shaw

GOD, I CAN'T WAIT FOR IT!*

I came to bring fire to the earth, and how I wish it were already kindled! I have a baptism with which to be baptized, and what stress I am under until it is completed!
—Luke 12:49–50

All wondrous creations—whether it is the creation of a baby, a new job, a new accomplishment, a new home, a new lifestyle, a new skill, a new relationship—all great creations must pass through a gestation period. All newborn gifts from God must be formed in the womb of God. But even this fetal period can be a precious gift for us to cherish if we allow it. That God would pour forth in our lives endless streams of new gifts to delight and renew us would be extraordinary enough to sing God's praises for all eternity. But God does more than that: God allows us to play *our part* in the creation of new things. God invites us to be cocreators. Indeed, *God's womb is inside us*: in our labor, in our dreams and visions, in our love for and with others, in our restlessness, in our dissatisfaction with the status quo and in our fortitude.

But any mother will tell you that pregnancies are tough. They require stamina and patience. Mothers-to-be know that the process cannot be rushed. The pregnant woman knows that after only a few weeks, she cannot say to her husband, "Oh, I just can't wait any longer: let's go have the baby now!" Mothers know this about babies, but so often the rest of us forget about the necessity of waiting for all of the other births in our lives. Our impatience and excitement will convince us that we do not have to wait any longer. Instead of cherishing each stage of

---

*Note: This entry addresses waiting for something good to happen. If you are waiting for something bad to happen, please see, "God, I'm Worried."

growth as a couple does with the kicks and tugs of their little one, we insist on inducing labor. We marry too quickly. We jump from job to job. We rush to the end of our tasks, compromising their quality. We move to the next step before perfecting the present one. And because our role as cocreators is not a mere token or sham—because God really does place this awesome responsibility in our hands—our "babies" often die of premature birth.

We must learn to wait. The old and weather-beaten cliché is right: good things really do come for those who wait. We must learn that getting there can be half the fun. Each moment of aching anticipation can be a celebration of the miracle of this new life springing forth (however slowly!). In prayer we must learn to sit quietly and place our spiritual ear beside the womb of God. And if we're quiet enough, we will feel the kick and hear the heartbeat of something new.

SUGGESTED SCRIPTURE PASSAGES

GENESIS 18:1–15: Abraham and Sarah are promised a child

2 KINGS 5:1–14: Naaman is healed of leprosy
after washing seven times

PSALM 107:4–9: The people are led into the Promised Land

ISAIAH 11:1–10: A shoot shall sprout from the stump of Jesse

ISAIAH 30:15–21: By waiting you shall be saved

ISAIAH 43:14–21: See, I am doing something new

ISAIAH 55:1–13: All who are thirsty, come to the water

ISAIAH 64:2–4: Eye has not seen what God has ready

JEREMIAH 29:11–14: I know the plans I have for you

MATTHEW 13:24–33: Parables about waiting

MATTHEW 25:1–13: The wise, waiting wedding guests

LUKE 1—2: Luke's Nativity narratives

LUKE 10:38–42: Martha, Martha, you are anxious
about many things

JOHN 20:11–18: Jesus appears to Mary Magdalene:
"I have not yet ascended"
JAMES 5:7–11: Wait for Christ's coming

PRAYER POINTERS

Whatever great thing I am awaiting, I imagine myself pregnant with this new creation. I ask God to help me to feel it kicking inside me and to hear a faint heartbeat. I celebrate the waiting.

I spend some prayer time merely praising God for the showering of gifts from heaven. I ask God to help me to focus on gratitude rather than impatience. I pray for those who lack the gifts I've been given and I reflect on how I might share my gifts with others.

I look for opportunities during the day to celebrate the gift of waiting: the line at the grocery store, the traffic jam, being put on hold, the wait for my late friend. I use these little moments to pray, thanking God for the gift for which I wait, regardless of how small that gift is.

I ask God to show me what he's up to when he makes me wait. I ask him to show me how I, myself, can grow and mature through waiting calmly and patiently.

I ask Jesus to show me how I might better prepare myself to be a steward of this gift, how I might reverently use this gift to advance the kingdom. I ask Jesus to show me also how I might misuse the gift, how I might take it for granted. I ask God for the wisdom and courage to receive, experience and share the gift according to the will of the Father.

RELATED ENTRIES

Content, Grateful, Joyful, Lost, Love, Morning

WORDS TO TAKE WITH YOU

You know that the beginning of any process is most important,
especially for anything young and tender. For it is at that time
that it takes shape, and any mold one may want can be
impressed upon it.
—Plato

There is no heavier burden than a great potential.
—Linus of *Peanuts*

Sometimes we have the dream but we are not ourselves ready
for the dream. We have to grow to meet it.
—Louis L'Amour, *Bendigo Shafter*

WAIT

GOD, I'M WEARY

> Then he said to me, "Prophesy to these bones, and say to them: O dry bones, hear the word of the LORD. Thus says the Lord GOD to these bones: I will cause breath to enter you, and you shall live. I will lay sinews on you, and will cause flesh to come upon you, and cover you with skin, and put breath in you, and you shall live; and you shall know that I am the LORD."
> —Ezekiel 37:4–6

This was in an E-mail my mom sent off to a group of her friends recently:

> I wanted to share a little experience I had with Michael, my four-year-old grandchild. He was at my home the other day and fell and scraped his hand. I quickly ran to him and said, "Oh, honey, did you get hurt?" He answered me in a very low painful way, "Yes, Granny, but it's OK. God will make me some more skin—he makes all the skin we need." ...One day, soon after that, I was experiencing a low, and I was reminded of the Scripture in Ezekiel 37 where it speaks of the "Dry Bones." I was really feeling like I was just dry bones that day. As I read the account, I came to verse 6, which says, "I will lay sinews on you, and will cause flesh to come upon you, and cover you with skin, and put breath in you, and you shall live; you shall know that I am the LORD." Life came into me at that moment as I reflected on that passage and also thought about what Michael had said, "God makes all the skin we need."

When I am weary or overwhelmed by life circumstances, there are three graces that I seek from God. First, I ask God to allow me to rest quietly in his arms. I actually imagine myself in Grandmother-God's rocking chair, having my wounds treated and hearing soft words of love whispered in my ear. This is probably what I need most from God right now. Second, I ask God to assure me that he will give me all the skin I need. My faith tells me that he will, of course, but when I'm overwhelmed by life, I need that reassurance from God in order to make it through another day. Like my nephew Michael, I can endure the wounds of today as long as I know that tomorrow God will begin to heal me and give me new skin. Finally, I ask God to breathe a new spirit into that new skin. Sometimes, burnout is when my true motives come home to roost. I may be feeling overwhelmed because somewhere along the way I have taken control of my life instead of daily turning my life back over to God. Weariness is a reminder that I cannot be the source of my own creative energy. Only if my spiritual lungs are filled with God's breath will I make it through another day. But by breathing God's spirit in—even in the midst of strife—it won't be long before I will take my new skins out for a dance in the desert.

WEARY

SUGGESTED SCRIPTURE PASSAGES

PSALM 131: Like a nursing child, so my soul is at rest
PSALM 137:1–6: There by the willows, we hung up our harps
ISAIAH 40:27–31: They shall run and not be weary
ISAIAH 55:1–13: All who are thirsty, come to the water
EZEKIEL 37:1–14: God revives dry bones
MATTHEW 11:28–30: Come to me all you who are weary
ROMANS 8:28–39: All things work together for the good
1 CORINTHIANS 1:4–9: You lack no spiritual gift
HEBREWS 12:5–13: So, strengthen your drooping hands
and weak knees

PRAYER POINTERS

I imagine God as my old but strong grandmother. I imagine myself as a small child exhausted from the little games I've played all day. I sit in Grandmother-God's lap, allowing her to rock me to a state of calm and peace. Together we sing some soft and slow song that soothes me.

In my imaginative prayer, I tell God all about my day. As I do so, I allow God to point out, at every step of the way, all the gifts I have been given to handle the situation. I am in awe and wonder at how wonderfully I've been made. I feel assured of my own ability to handle all of the work of my life.

Looking back on my day, I go to the most difficult part of it and see how God was present there, even though I probably did not recognize him at the time. I thank God for his strong presence in my life and have a conversation with him about it.

I slow down my breathing. I ask God to breathe his Spirit within me. As I exhale, I imagine breathing out all the troubles and worries of my life. As I inhale, I imagine breathing in the soothing, calming Spirit of God. I praise God for the fresh air of his Spirit, and I surrender my life to God's care.

RELATED ENTRIES

Busy, Ministry, Parenting, Procrastinator, Sad, Stressed

WORDS TO TAKE WITH YOU

God gives us all the skin we need.
—Michael Thibodeaux

GOD, I'M WORRIED

What then are we to say about these things? If God is for us, who is against us? He who did not withhold his own Son, but gave him up for all of us, will he not with him also give us everything else?...Who will separate us from the love of Christ? Will hardship, or distress, or persecution, or famine, or nakedness, or peril, or sword?...

No, in all these things we are more than conquerors through him who loved us. For I am convinced that neither death, nor life, nor angels, nor rulers, nor things present, nor things to come, nor powers, nor height, nor depth, nor anything else in all creation, will be able to separate us from the love of God in Christ Jesus our Lord.
—Romans 8:31–32, 35, 37–39

Sometimes worry is irrational. I remember one day counseling a very bright high school student who told me, through tears, that he worried about flunking out of school. Going through his grades with him, I was able to show him that there was practically no way he would fail. He saw that the fear was an irrational one and worried much less about it from then on.

Sometimes worry is quite rational. If a friend's personality suddenly and dramatically shifts for the worse, it is reasonable to be worried about this. Worry can be a healthy emotion, then, because it points to legitimate areas of concern in my life.

If I enter prayer worried about something, I must first ask myself, "Is it reasonable for me to be so worried about this?" If my heart tells me "yes" but in my mind I know that it's silly for me to be so preoccupied, then—in the same way that I consoled my young student—my head must gently and lovingly explain to my heart why there is no reason to get upset. Researchers in psychology have shown that when we talk to ourselves, we really do listen! For example, if I tell myself every day that I am ugly, I will gradually begin to feel ugly. Likewise, if in prayer I allow my rational mind to present evidence that my present fear is irrational, then after a while, my heart will begin to believe it, too.

My next step in prayer would be to allow Jesus to work on my deeper insecurities. I imagine Jesus with his arm around me as I reveal to him the part of me that is so frightened of the world. I allow Jesus to look me in the eye and say, "I will be with you always, Mark. You have nothing to fear." I could use this as a mantra in my prayer.

On the other hand, if my worry is rational, if there is good reason to be concerned about this, then I ask Jesus in my prayer to be with me as I sit in this unhappy state of worry. I ask Jesus to make his presence felt to me in a tangible way so that I might use his presence as the security blanket of my soul. In my prayer I could imagine myself in every possible scenario that could occur, and in each one I see and feel Jesus standing right beside me with his hand on my shoulder. I hear Jesus in those moments whispering in my ear, "I am with you always." Knowing that Jesus is at my side, I am ready to face even the worst of circumstances.

SUGGESTED SCRIPTURE PASSAGES

PSALM 6: Prayer in time of distress
PSALM 23: The Lord is my shepherd, I shall not want
PSALM 118: The Lord is with me; I fear not
ISAIAH 25:4—26:4: The Lord is an eternal rock
ISAIAH 43:1–8: When you walk through fire,
you shall not be burned
JEREMIAH 29:11–14: I know the plans I have for you
JOEL 2:15—3:2: Call to penance; the Lord responds
MATTHEW 6:25–34: Consider the lilies
MATTHEW 10:16–20: Don't worry about what to say

MATTHEW 14:22–33: Jesus rescues the apostles
from the stormy sea
MATTHEW 28:16–20: I am with you to the end
MARK 5:21–43: Fear is useless—what is needed is faith
LUKE 10:38–42: Martha, Martha, you are anxious
about many things
LUKE 12:22–34: Do not worry about your life
LUKE 22:40–46: Jesus sweats blood in the garden of
Gethsemane
ROMANS 8:28–39: All things work together for the good
2 CORINTHIANS 12:7–10: My grace is sufficient for you
PHILIPPIANS 4:4–9: Do not worry about anything

PRAYER POINTERS

In my imagination I see myself going through the worst-case scenario of what might happen. I watch the ugly scene as though watching myself in a movie. But I notice that through it all, Jesus is standing just behind me with his hand on my shoulder, whispering in my ear, "Do not be afraid, Mark, I am with you."

I draw a picture of the above scene paying close attention to Jesus' hand, to his eyes, to the expression on his face.

On paper I describe in detail the worst-case scenario. In my prayer I read this description aloud. But after each sentence I say, "But you are with me, Lord." For example, my prayer might go something like this:

My girlfriend gets angry with me. *But you are with me, Lord.*
She yells and screams at me. *But you are with me, Lord.*
I feel hurt and rejected. *But you are with me, Lord.*
I try to talk to her, but she doesn't listen. *But you are with me, Lord.*
She dumps me and I am alone. *But you are with me, Lord.*

RELATED ENTRIES

Afraid, Change, Despair, Nighttime, Parenting, Stressed

WORDS TO TAKE WITH YOU

"Come to the edge," he said.
"We'll fall," they said.
"Come to the edge," he said.
They came; he pushed them...
They flew.
—from an AIDS quilt panel made by
high school students for their deceased teacher

Worrying is like rocking in a rocking chair: it gives you
something to do, but it doesn't get you anywhere.
—Glenn Turner

Worry often gives a small thing a big shadow.
—Swedish Proverb

INDEX OF THEMES

Find the entry that best fits your mood or situation
and look it up in the Table of Contents.

HAPPY MOODS AND SITUATIONS

Awe of Your Creation

Thank You for My Body

Perfectly Content

Grateful

Joyful

In Love

Proud

Still and Quiet

Can't Wait

PRAYING THROUGH YOUR DAY

Morning

Noontime

Evening

Nighttime

VOCATIONS

Family

Marriage

Ministry

Parenting

Single Life

ANGER AND BAD FEELINGS ABOUT OTHERS

Angry
Angry at You
Blew Up Today
Can't Forgive
Hate Myself
Hurt
Jealous

FEAR AND DOUBTS

Afraid
Change
Despair
Doubts

DIFFICULT MOODS AND EMOTIONS

Spiritually Dry
Grieving
Lonely
Lost
Sad
Weary

DIFFICULT SITUATIONS

Busy
Confront
Decide
Dying
Sexually Aroused
Stressed Out
Worried

SIN
Addicted
Guilty
Bad Habits
In Lust
Judgmental
Procrastinator
Sinfully Proud
Sinned

INDEX OF OTHER EMOTIONS AND SITUATIONS

If you can't find an entry for your mood,
try one of these alternatives:

If you're feeling:	Look up:
I'm Alone	Lonely
I Feel Alienated	Hurt, Lonely
I Feel Ambivalent	Decide, Lost
I'm Angry at Myself	Hate Myself
I'm Anxious	Worried
I'm Arrogant	Judgmental, Proud
I'm Ashamed	Guilty, Hate Myself, Sinned
I Feel Beautiful	Body
Help Me to Believe	Doubts
I Feel Betrayed	Forgive, Hurt
I'm Bored	Dry, Procrastinator
I'm Burned Out	Stressed, Weary
I Feel Called	Ministry
I Feel Cheated	Hurt
I Need Clarity	Decide, Lost
I'm Closed-Hearted	Hate Myself, Sinned

I'm Ready to Commit	Marriage, Ministry
I Need Compassion	Forgive, Ministry
I'm Competitive	Judgmental, Proud
I Feel Complacent	Dry, Procrastinator
I'm Concerned	Afraid, Worried
I Need Confidence	Afraid, Hate Self
I Feel Conflicted	Decide, Lost
I'm Confused	Decide, Lost
I Need Courage	Afraid
I Feel Cranky	Angry
I Need Creativity	Dry, Procrastinator
I've Been Criticized	Hurt
I Need to Detach	Confront, Parenting
I Need to Discern	Decide, Lost
I Feel Defeated	Hurt, Grieving
I'm Defiant	Angry, Forgive
I'm Depressed	Lonely, Sad
I'm Desperate	Despair, Worried
I Feel Detached	Lonely, Sad
I'm Devastated	Sad, Weary
I Need Direction	Decide, Lost
I Feel Discouraged	Grieving, Sad
I'm Excited about It!	Can't Wait, Joyful,
I'm Exhausted	Stressed, Weary
I Need Faith	Doubts, Dry
Friendship Is Tough!	Marriage, Family
I've Lost a Friend	Grieving, Hurt
I'm Frightened	Afraid, Worried
I'm Frustrated	Angry, Stressed
I'm Furious	Angry, Forgive
I'm Gluttonous	Habits, Sinned
I'm Greedy	Habits, Sinned
I'm Grumpy	Angry, Noontime

I'm Happy with Myself	Joyful, Proud
I Hate My Body	Body, Hate Myself
I'm in Need of Healing	Hurt, Sad
I Just Wanted to Say Hi	Content, Morning
I Feel Honored	Grateful, Proud
I Feel Hopeless	Sad, Weary
I'm Horny	Lust, Sexually Aroused
I'm Hungry for You	Dry, Lonely, Quiet
I Need Integrity	Sinned, Confront
I Need to Let Go	Grieving, Parenting
I Feel Liberated	Grateful, Joyful
I Long for You	Dry, Quiet, Lonely
I Love Myself	Grateful, Proud
I Feel Your Love for Me	Awe, Content, Quiet
I Feel Loved by Others	Content, Grateful
I'm Moody	Angry, Noontime
I'm Needy	Addicted, Nighttime
I'm Offended	Forgive, Hurt
I'm Out of Control	Addicted, Blew Up
I Feel Out-of-Sorts	Lonely, Sad
I'm Overwhelmed	Despair, Stressed
I'm in Pain	Hurt, Sad
I'm in Panic	Despair, Nighttime
I Need Patience	Angry, Noontime
I'm a Perfectionist	Habits, Weary
I Need Perseverance	Ministry, Weary
I Don't Feel Like Praying	Angry, Dry
I'm Prejudiced	Judgmental
I've Been Persecuted	Hurt, Ministry
I Can't Feel Your Presence	Angry, Dry
I Need Your Protection	Afraid, Nighttime
I Feel Relieved	Grateful, Morning
I'm Resigned to It	Change, Confront

I Feel Resistant	Change, Doubts
I Need to Rest in You	Quiet, Stressed
I'm Restless	Lonely, Can't Wait
I Said Something Stupid	Blew Up, Habits
I'm Scared	Afraid, Nighttime
I've Been Self-Destructive	Addicted, Hate Myself
I Have Low Self-Esteem	Hate Myself, Lust
I Feel Called to Service	Ministry, Single
I'm in Shock	Despair, Grieving
I Can't Sleep	Nighttime, Worried
I Need Stillness	Quiet, Stressed
I Feel Stupid	Guilty, Hate Myself
I'm Suffering	Hurt, Sad
I'm Terrified	Afraid, Despair
I'm Thrilled	Joyful, Can't Wait
I'm Tired	Stressed, Weary
I'm in Transition	Change, Can't Wait
I Feel Trapped	Despair, Lost
Help Me to Trust	Doubts
I Feel Ugly	Body, Hate Self
I'm Uncertain	Decide, Lost
I'm Undecided	Decide
I'm Underappreciated	Hurt, Lonely
I Need Understanding	Decide, Lost
I'm Unhappy	Sad
I Feel Unlovable	Hate Myself
I Feel Unloved	Hate Myself, Lonely
I'm Upset	Angry, Despair
I Feel Used	Angry, Hurt
I've Been Victimized	Forgive, Hurt
I Long for Wisdom	Decide, Lost
I Yearn for You	Loneliness
I Feel Rejected	Angry, Hurt